God in My Kitchen

Fifty-two Thoughts for Homemakers

By

DOROTHY C. HASKIN

WARNER PRESS
Anderson, Indiana

Second Printing, 1958
Third Printing, 1959
Fourth Printing, 1960

Acknowledgments

The kitchen shown on the cover was designed by Home Guide, Inc., using General Electric appliances. We are indebted to these organizations for the picture. The poems by Martha Snell Nicholson are used by permission of Moody Press. Some of these devotionals appeared originally in *Christian Parent, Evangel, The Lutheran, The Beacon and Evangelist, The Standard,* and *Youth's Christian Companion.*

Library of Congress
Catalog Card Number 58-6418

PRINTED IN THE UNITED STATES OF AMERICA

How to Use This Book

This book ought to feel at home around the kitchen. In the first place, it is addressed to those who make homes and deals in concise fashion with many matters of the religious faith of concern to such people. Then, too, with its plastic cover and spiral binding it can be used conveniently right in the kitchen, the "heart" of most homes.

The selections are short, designed for quick reading. They may well lead the reader into longer paths of meditation and Bible reading. It happens that there are fifty-two such selections, one for each week of the year, if you are the systematic kind of reader who would like to go straight through and use each selection as the theme for thinking for a week.

On the other hand, if you aren't interested in that approach, you may read the selections at random and at your own pace. As you become familiar with the book, you will know what sections to pick to match your need, your mood, or the time of year. We wish you fruitful reading and meditation, perhaps as you wait to take a cake out of the oven or during a quiet period just after you have sent the youngsters off to school.

—The Editors

Contents

Page

1 The Bible Bound in You

Three men were talking about some of the recent translations of the Bible. One said, "I like that Phillips version of the Gospels. It's easy reading. The Berkeley isn't bad either."

"Maybe," the second man shrugged his shoulders. "But believe me, nothing compares with the King James Version."

"I know a better one," the third man said.

"What one do you mean?"

"I like my mother's translation best. She translated the Bible into life and it was the most convincing translation I ever saw."

The man was right! There is no more convincing version of the Bible than the one which is lived. As the Lord Jesus said, "Ye shall be witnesses unto me" (Acts 1:8). It does not matter if you want to be or not, the Christian is His witness. Some of us are poor witnesses. Others are inspiring witnesses. Either way, the sign that hung in a college YMCA is still true:

> "Be careful how you live; you may be the only Bible some people will ever read."

Or, as someone phrased it,

> "More people read the Bible bound in shoe leather than they do bound in morocco."

A well-translated life centered on the teachings of the Bible gives much light. People so living are like the windows the little girl saw. For the first time in her life, she visited one of the large cathedrals in a big city where she saw the magnificent stained glass windows with the golden sun pouring through the colored glass. The child, noticing the figures on the glass windows, asked, "Auntie, who are the people on the beautiful windows?"

"They are saints," her aunt told her.

"Oh," the child exclaimed, "now I know what saints are! They are the people who let the light shine through."

An apt definition! Christ is the light of the world and only as we let his light shine through our lives, our acts, our words, are we living up to the fullest and finest for him.

It follows that the slightest thing in front of a window cuts off some of the light of the sun. Even a flimsy curtain cuts off its share of light. Every failure, every unkindness, every thoughtless word spoken by a Christian cheats children, friends, acquaintances, of a little of the light of Christ.

What a challenge to live and pray each day, "Let the beauty of Jesus be seen in me."

2 The Acid Test

A testimony meeting was being held in the South by J. M. Buckley, a visiting minister. One woman arose and told how much comfort her religion gave her in times of trouble.

"That's fine, Sister," commented Dr. Buckley. "But how about the practical side? Does your religion make you strive to prepare your husband a good dinner? Does it make you keep his socks darned?"

Just then Dr. Buckley felt a yank at his coattails. It was the local pastor, who whispered, "Press them questions, Doctor, press them questions. That's my wife."

Yes, "press them questions" to yourself. The acid test of your religion is not that it makes you comfortable, but that it helps you make others comfortable. He "comforteth us in all our tribulation, that we may be able to comfort them which are in any trouble" (II Cor. 1:4). Often, it is such a little thing which proves our religion to others.

A soldier was on leave in Paris during World War II. He was eager to get a good meal and to see the sights. But he saw, getting off the train, an old lady, poorly dressed, carrying three heavy bags. As there were no porters available, he helped her to the subway; then, seeing she could not possibly manage with the bags, he gave up his plans for a pleasant evening. He boarded the train and rode with her to her home in the suburbs. The gratitude of the woman left a lasting impression on the young man. He saw the need of giving a "cup of cold water" in Christ's name.

Yet, how many people actually put themselves out for others? So imbedded in us is the idea that to help others is an annoyance, that even when we ask someone to pass something at the table, we say, "May I bother you?"

"Pure religion and undefiled before God and the Father is this, To visit the fatherless and widows in their affliction" (Jas. 1:27). Pure religion prompts you—

To give Dad a more welcome greeting than the dog gives him, when he comes home.

To know if the postman's wife is sick.

To put the hymnals back in the rack to save the janitor work.

To speak kindly to your naughty little boy.

To iron the dress for your sister.

To listen to the troubles of another.

To give away not the unwanted dress but the one you might wear again.

To remind the Sunday school superintendent that Mrs. Smith might like to teach.

To help paint the church basement.

To make benches for the beginners' department.

To call the elevator man by his name.

To be on time for appointments.

The acid test is not, "What does my religion do for me?" but, "What does it make me do for others?"

3 Beauty

A girl was so violently jealous of her sister that she was taken to see a minister well-known for his spiritual counsel. It was hoped that he would be able to help her. To him, she raved against her sister, telling how popular her sister was, how her sister outshone her, and how unhappy she herself was as a result.

The minister decided he should meet the younger sister. He expected to see a beautiful girl and was surprised to find she was plain but had a friendly spirit and inner beauty of character.

True beauty is not skin deep as the old saying goes. Rather, it is beneath the skin. Washington Irving realized, "It is the divinity within that makes the divinity without."

Sheer physical good looks do not necessarily go together with excelling character or outstanding achievement. Our most handsome presidents were perhaps Warren G. Harding, James Buchanan, Franklin Pierce, and Chester A. Arthur. None of these are rated by historians as among our top national leaders. The presidents most praised by historians were not handsome men. George Washington was pock-marked. Abraham Lincoln's rugged features are well-known and Theodore Roosevelt was bristling in appearance. Parents will do well to mention these things, because many children worry about their looks.

Beauty is something which every girl can have. A young girl was praised for her beauty. Privately her father told her, "People are not praising your beauty, but your youth. You can take no credit at all for beauty at sixteen. But if you are beautiful at sixty, you can be proud of it, for it will be your character which has made you beautiful."

True beauty shows when the face is in repose. The natural expression reflects the character. It may be fretty, quarrelsome, or reveal a spirit at rest in God. Another time that true beauty may be seen is when you greet someone. If you are self-centered, your greeting is without feeling and does not light your face. But if you are genuinely friendly, your greeting of others will bring a radiance to your face.

A Quaker woman's recipe for beauty was:

> "Use for the lips, truth . . . for the voice, prayer . . . for the eyes, pity . . . for the hands, charity . . . for the figure, uprightness . . . and for the heart, love."

Robert McCheyne was a saintly man of God, who, in his comparatively short life, won many souls to the Lord. After he died, a letter addressed to him was found on his desk. It was from a person he had led to Christ and said, "It was nothing you said that first made me wish to be a Christian. It was the beauty of holiness which I saw in your face."

4 "Let's Not Read the Bible"

D. L. Moody said that when he was a young man he would hoe a field of corn so poorly that the next morning he could not tell where he had stopped. And some people read the Bible in the same manner. They read it casually and carelessly, as if it were an essay on philosophy or a collection of wise sayings.

But it is not. It brings us God's Word, and because of this it should be studied. "Study to show thyself approved unto God" (II Tim. 2:15). So this year, let's not merely read the Bible; let's *study* it.

Take one book, such as one of the Epistles, and read it every day until you actually know what it says. Read it until, without looking at the Bible, you can write a summary of it. Read whatever commentaries you can on the book. Memorize the outstanding verses.

Or, select one of the Psalms and read it every day for a month.

Reading aloud will help you concentrate on what you are reading. If you have a cross reference Bible, look up the references. Read the footnotes. Read any parallel passages which come to your mind. Write your own cross references in the margin.

By reading or meditating on one portion of the Bible for a month, you will learn more of the Lord and his Word than by merely reading the whole Bible for a year.

But most of all, obey whatever the Word says. "Behold, to obey is better than sacrifice, and to hearken than the fat of rams" (I Sam. 15:22).

Read your portion for the day until a verse impresses you; then stop reading and think about it. If no verse impresses you, stop at the end of the chapter and think through the entire portion. The fact that you didn't respond to it may indicate that you need this passage more than any other.

Ask yourself, "Is there something in this passage that I should obey?"

"Is there something for which I should pray?"

"Does it point out a sin for me to avoid?"

Find the lesson and apply it to yourself. Make is practical by obeying it. It is all too easy to say *Yes* to God and not mean it.

Upon the assembly floor of the British Columbia Native Brotherhood the question came up, "When does an Indian mean 'No'?" An old chief, sitting at the back, rose to his full height and said, "It is very simple when Indian mean 'No.' When Indian say 'Yes' and do nothing, Indian mean 'No'."

Any person who reads the Word of God and does nothing, is saying *No* to God. This year, let's not merely read the Bible; let's study it and obey it.

5 The Best Years of Her Life

Lady Grizel Hume Baille said the best years of her life were the ones she spent in Holland. She lived during the seventeenth century and her family was persecuted for its religious beliefs. When she was in her teens her family had fled from Scotland to Holland to escape religious persecution.

There the family lived in extreme poverty. Every morning before six, Grizel lit the fire in her father's study, woke up the family and prepared breakfast. Then, while her father taught the younger children, she went to the market, took the corn to the mill to be ground, cleaned the house, mended clothes and cooked dinner. Her older brother had only one change of linen and she often stayed up at night to wash and iron it for him.

They were the best years of her life because they called forth the best that was in Grizel.

Others, too, have had hard times or suffered handicaps, the very thing which brought out the best that was in them. Helen Keller was born a bright and normal baby. When she was eighteen months old she caught the dreadful scarlet fever which took away both her sight and hearing. She soon forgot the few words she had learned and tried by means of signs to tell her mother what was going on in her mind. When she was hungry, she stood at the table and pretended to cut bread and spread butter on it.

When she was six years old, her father took her to see Alexander Graham Bell, the inventor and teacher of the deaf and dumb. He suggested the father hire a teacher from the school for the blind in Boston. Anne Sullivan came to teach Helen and slowly Helen learned to spell out words, to read, and even in time to talk.

She graduated from Radcliffe College and became internationally known. She has lectured widely, traveling in this country and many others. She has brought help and courage to the blind throughout the world. She says, "I thank God for my handicaps; for through them I have found myself, my work, and my God."

It was when the Apostle Paul was in a Roman prison, when he was stripped of his liberty, when he was chained to a Roman soldier, that he wrote the epistle to the Philippians. The epistle rings with joy. Paul had triumphed over his hardship.

"Kites rise against, not with the wind."

6 The Biggest Job in the World

"My mother always cooked rice with chicken fricassee, and so I prefer it that way," said Nancy to her young husband.

"Is that so?" he frowned. "My mother always had chicken and noodles, and I prefer it that way."

"All right, we'll have it my way one time and yours the next and our children will learn to like chicken cooked both ways," Nancy decided.

In those few sentences was expressed one of the basic truths of life: We like what we are taught to like by our parents . . . we react as we are taught to react by our parents . . . we are, to a large extent, what we are, because of the way our parents did or did not obey. "Train up a child in the way he should go: and when he is old, he will not depart from it" (Prov. 22:6).

Long after the child becomes an adult he continues to behave as if still in the home of his parents because a series of reaction patterns have been set up. Dora has always been afraid of her mild-mannered husband because her mother was a stern woman. Charles accepted his wife's working, as a matter of course, because his mother had always worked to help support the family.

Mothers have just about the biggest job in the world because they shape their children physically, mentally, and spiritually.

Pauline often complains because her daughter Gwen isn't neat. But why should Gwen be neat? There is never a time when you can enter Pauline's home and not see dirty dishes standing on the sink. And while Pauline keeps the top of her dresser tidy, she stuffs things in the drawer. Though Pauline nags, nagging will not teach Gwen to be neat.

Bob resents the fact that his two daughters don't help their mother in the kitchen though she works every day to help support them. He feels his daughters should appreciate their mother more, but he reads the paper while his wife washes the dinner dishes. He doesn't stir to help her and the daughters are so accustomed to seeing their mother carry the heavy end that they follow their father's example and let her carry it.

Mr. Tittell was a farmer. He said that since he never knew exactly what his income was, he couldn't tithe. His son works in the city and knows exactly how much he earns, but he doesn't see the use of tithing.

The records of the China Inland Mission show many third- and fourth-generation missionaries serving with them. This is true of other mission and church agencies.

Being a mother or father is a tremendous job. Because of their influence on the child they must constantly strive to grow mentally and spiritually. Only as the parent is his best, will the child be the best possible person.

7 Circles or Spirals

Mary Jordan stood at the front door of her home in the small midwestern community and watched her oldest boy Ted hurry his little sister Alicia down the street. Off to school for another year.

Each year the first day of school brought mingled feelings to Mary. Relief, that the house would be quiet for a few hours and she would get something done . . . but sadness, too, because each time the children went to school, they went farther and farther from her.

She thought as she walked slowly back into the kitchen, gathering the dishes off the breakfast table and taking them to the sink. "Someday they'll graduate. They'll be through school. They'll have learned their lessons, while I. . . ." She glanced away from her work, out of the window. "Lord, don't I ever learn? It seems as if I go through the same lessons over and over again."

This past summer there had been the horrible polio scare when she had hugged her children close to her heart and prayed in frantic half sentences. It seemed as if she had been more upset than the year before, when the polio scare had hit the community. And there had been the night when her husband had helped a neighbor with his broken-down car without phoning her. She had prayed. That is, she had prayed until the last half hour before Fred came home. Then she had worried. She wondered, "Lord, will I ever learn? I just seem to go in circles."

Not only Mary Jordan but many other Christians feel as if they go in circles. Even as far back as the children of Israel, there were those who felt that they went in circles. When they went out from Egypt, it is said that they were eleven days' journey from Kadesh-barnea, the entrance to the Promised Land.

However, because of their wanderings, the first time that they arrived at Kadesh-barnea was about the fifth month of the second year. There they received the discouraging reports from spies sent into the Promised Land. They had not learned the lesson of faith and so they continued wandering in and around in circles. The next time they reached Kadesh-barnea they were in the fortieth year of their journeying, but this time they went into the land of Canaan. They had learned the lesson of faith.

All of us have a Kadesh-barnea in our lives, a place where we have to learn to trust God regardless of the circumstances in our lives. All too often when we reach this place, we pray to get out of it instead of praying to learn the lesson of the place.

Florence has recurring attacks of sinus. Each time they come her cry is for healing that she may live for the glory of God. But God neither heals nor shows her a way to be healed. Therefore, it is obvious that patience with sinus is one lesson she must learn to the glory of God. Patricia has the numb sorrow of being married to a man who is unresponsive to her interests. Once they separated. But while Patricia enjoyed the freedom, she knew it was not God's way. They were united and now when the marriage seems too confining a prison, Patricia prays, "Teach me to live rightly within it." And while the marriage still lacks unity, Patricia does face conditions with greater wisdom. Patricia has learned:

We don't walk in circles—we walk in spirals.

We will meet the problem often until we learn to face it in His peace and joy. Then we'll reach the top of the spiral.

8 Dishwashing Devotions

Eloise was a highly educated young girl, trained in music and the world's finest literature. But when she went to summer camp she had to take her turn at K.P. duty.

She was peeling potatoes when someone remarked,

"It is too bad that a girl with your ability has to spend her time peeling potatoes."

Eloise glanced up and smiled, "But when I peel potatoes I don't have to think about them. I can think about the Lord."

She knew a secret of being happy while working in the kitchen. It is thinking of things above. A man known as Brother Lawrence learned it many years ago. He was a footman for a noble family in France. But he decided that he wanted to serve God. He became a monk, expecting, no doubt, to be given some noble task to do. Instead, he was assigned to work in the kitchen.

At first he thought he could not stand it. The work was distasteful to him. But gradually, as he peeled potatoes, washed the dishes, and even as he did the shopping for the monastery, he began to think of God. In time he could say, "The time of business does not with me differ from the time of prayer; and in the noise and clatter of my kitchen, while several persons are at the same time calling for different things, I possess God in as great tranquillity as if I were upon my knees at the altar."

He had learned the great secret of "practicing the presence of God." He had learned it so thoroughly that he wrote his friends about his joy in serving God in the kitchen. After his death his letters were collected and printed in book form. They have gone through many editions and been translated in English. Immortal fame came to this humble man who spent many years of his life in the kitchen because he learned that as he worked he could think of God.

Many women have also learned the secret of rising above the monotony of housework. One person I know has memorized many chapters of the Bible. While she vacuums, she repeats the chapters from memory and they warm her heart. Another friend of mine keeps a poem in a plastic frame over her sink, and as she washes dishes she memorizes the poem.

Beds have to be made. Dishes have to be washed. There is no way to avoid housework; while your hands do automatic tasks, your thoughts can be on God and your life be filled with joy.

9 Does Your Child Think You Are a Christian?

Gwen paused at the front door and nervously tightened the green scarf about her neck. The house was so still. Doug had stopped sobbing and she could still see him stretched out on his bed, his fists clenched. With all the fierceness of a thirteen-year-old boy, he had hissed, "Yah, go to choir. When you sing, can't nobody tell how mean you are."

Of course, he was wrong. She wasn't mean. She had been perfectly right to scold him. He had stayed out playing after dark when she had repeatedly told him to come home the minute the street lights were turned on. But could she go to choir practice when he thought her a hypocrite?

She caught a glimpse of her face in the mirror over the fireplace. She did look cross. She sighed as through her mind floated fragments of Scripture: "the servant of the Lord must not strive; but be gentle unto all" (II Tim. 2:24). "Let your speech be always with grace" (Col. 4:6). But did they apply to one's child?

Gwen knew they did. She had to scold her son, not as a rasping harpy but rather as a self-controlled Christian. She went back into her son's room to talk to him, knowing, "I'll be late for choir practice but I have a responsibility to my family."

Over and over in Scripture the Christian's responsibility to his family is emphasized. "But if any provide not for his own, and specially for those of his own house, he hath denied the faith" (I Tim. 5:8). Check your Christian testimony as it must appear to your child:

1. Have you ever (a) talked to your child about commiting himself to Christ, or (b) do you think that is the minister's responsibility (Deut. 4:9)?

2. Do you expect your child (a) to have a child's judgment, or (b) do you expect, because he comes from a Christian home, that he will have mature judgment (I Cor. 13:11)?

3. Do you (a) discipline your child, or (b) do you feel it is better to simply pray about the discipline problem (Heb. 12:7)?

4. Do you (a) severely punish your son, or (b) do you remember your own childhood (Eph. 6:4)?

5. If your son breaks his arm, do you (a) lament the additional bills, or (b) look upon the experience as an opportunity for your son to learn patience (Rom. 8:28)?

To the first three questions the better answer is of course "a"—to the last two, "b." No place does our Christian conduct receive the "work out" that it does at home. It is God's testing ground for us. But living our Christian testimony at home is worth-while. Bruce became a prominent businessman and politician. He was especially known for his clean politics. He was asked, "How come you live as square as you do?"

"I'm a Christian," he replied.

"In this day and age, when you hear so much unbelief?"

"Men can talk but my mother lived what she believed and no argument is stronger than a mother who lives for Christ."

10 Find the Time

Elizabeth Fry could not even take the time to complain that she didn't have time to help others. She had eleven children and the responsibilities of a large home. But she lived in England in an age when there were two hundred crimes for which a man might be hung. The expression, "I might as well be hung for a sheep as a lamb," originated in those days because it was the truth.

All prisoners, convicted or not convicted, were locked in the same cell—whether their crime be murder or a minor offense. The women brought their children with them. The prisoners were given straw for a bed; their food had to be brought to them by their friends; and their days were spent in idleness.

When Elizabeth heard about these conditions, she decided to do something about it and so went to the jail. The jailer refused to let her into the women's cell, afraid they might attack her and steal her watch. But Elizabeth had obtained permission from the governor of Newgate Prison to go in and she insisted on doing so.

Once inside, she won the women's hearts by picking up a filthy child and saying, "Women, do you want your children to grow up and become real prisoners as you are?"

"No," they shouted. So, Elizabeth and the women made plans. She taught them to sew so that they might earn a living when released. She arranged for a teacher for the children and she herself read the Bible to them.

Elizabeth Fry found time to help others because she knew God would have her do it. Her first thought on waking in the morning was, "What can I do today for Jesus?"

All of us have more time than we realize. A reporter interviewed a self-made man. He asked, "You have educated yourself while you fought your way to success. Tell me, how did you do your reading during those busy years?"

"It is quite simple," the man explained. "I kept a good book open on my desk, and whenever someone on the phone said, 'Just a moment,' I read my book."

And there are other spare moments. A friend of mine knits an average of five pairs of wristlets a year for the patients in a TB sanitarium. She only knits when she is waiting for a streetcar, or when riding in their automobile with her husband driving. Take a look a your life. If you wish to help others you will find that there is time.

11 The March Winds Do Blow!

The young girl in the hospital bed fussed at the nurse, at the doctor, at her visitors. They were patient, trying to comfort her but she would not be comforted. The north wind of life had blown upon her and drawn out only bitterness. If she had had greater inner resources, she might have said, "Awake, O north wind; and come, thou south; blow upon my garden, that the spices thereof may flow out. Let my beloved come in his garden, and eat his pleasant fruits" (Song of Sol. 4:16).

When the March winds blow upon a life the Lord intends that they shall draw out of us the best.

The north wind of poverty blew upon Mrs. Stewart for many years. Her husband died accidentally, shortly before her fifth child was born. It was during the depression years, but she valiantly faced the task of supporting her family with a meager income, earned by doing washing and ironing for others. Her problems were enough to embitter another woman. The children were normal and chafed under the constant denial. During their teen years they were thoughtless of their mother. But the strength and sweetness of her character poured upon the household, quieting the rebellion of her children. Now that they are grown, they are happy and normal because the north wind could blow upon their mother and bring out the best.

The north wind of sickness has blown for over forty years on Martha Snell Nicholson. Most of those years she has been confined to her home, for long periods of time to her room. But she has accepted her weakness with fortitude. The pungentness of allspice has come from her life and her pen. She has blessed the world, not with a Pollyanna gladness but with a creative acceptance of her role in life. As she wrote to express her feelings:

> I do not ask that Thou wilt take this pain away,
> But, Father, may I bear no fruitless pain today!
>
> I do not plead that Thou wilt wipe away my tears,
> But rather, may I see, throughout the passing years,
>
> Watered by tears of mine, some fragrant blossoms start
> Within the barren desert of another's heart.

The north wind of living with a trying relative blew upon Kathryn's garden. Cramped by living with an aging father, whose belief in Christ was more like fire insurance for a coming world than an annuity for this world, she was deprived of many things. She could not go freely with those of her own age to parties and programs. She could not spend money for clothes to make herself more attractive. But she accepted the limitations set upon her life with the pungentness of nutmeg.

She had a gay word for her father's complaining. She had a cheery refusal when invitations came. She managed to make many of her clothes and household things . . . there was a collar made from an old slip . . . there was a lamp shade made from a scarf. She did not wait for her father's death to be happy. She was happy now. She sang:

Let the beauty of Jesus be seen in me,
All His wonderful passion and purity;
O Thou Spirit divine, all my nature refine,
Till the beauty of Jesus is seen in me.

The March winds do blow, that June may come.

12 The Courage of Easter

Ronny thought his friend's folks acted so odd. It was during World War I. Ronny was an American and in the trenches in France he met Bert, an Englishman. When Ronny was able to get a few days' furlough, Bert suggested he visit his parents in England. That pleased Ronny and so he crossed the Channel and went to the pleasant town, to Bert's home.

It was then he thought Bert's parents acted queer. They welcomed him, all right. They apparently wanted him to enjoy his few days of rest and furlough. But they refused to discuss Bert. He had thought they would want to talk about him, hear what a splendid soldier he was. Instead, any time he brought up the subject of Bert, either his father or mother changed the subject or left the room.

Two days after his arrival was Easter Sunday. He went to church with the parents. It was a stately stone church and the service was formal. Ronny wasn't quite at ease. He was used to a more Americanized service. But the flowers on the altar were beautiful and he enjoyed the Easter message. The Scripture, "I am the resurrection, and the life: he that believeth in me, though he were dead, yet shall he live" (John 11:25), was comforting to a man who, the next day, was to return to the trenches to face death.

After the services, as Ronny and Bert's parents walked along the country road, they seemed relaxed and a gentle smile played on Bert's mother's face. The father explained, "It's been a fine service. Ronny, I suppose we've given you quite a time. But you see, while you were crossing the Channel, Bert's number came up. . . ."

"No!" Ronny instinctively exclaimed.

"And that was why we didn't want to talk about Bert," the father continued. "We felt we couldn't face it."

"But the service this morning gave us the courage," the mother said.

This glad story of Easter has been repeated in the hearts of many parents. Death is no respecter of persons. It comes to the crib, to the teen-ager, and to the aged. It brings always the sorrow of parting. It matters not if the dying one goes suddenly, or has been expected to go; sorrow is always there.

There is no real solace to death but Easter. One glorious morning three women went to a garden tomb and found it empty. No other religion in the world ends on that happy note—the empty tomb! The men in shining garments said, "Why seek ye the living among the dead? He is not here, but is risen" (Luke 24:5, 6).

Since that dew-laden morning, each year hope is renewed as Christians gather to sing the songs of Easter, to hear again the promise, "Because I live, ye shall live also" (John 14:19). All our hopes of tomorrow rest in the action of yesterday. "I the Lord have spoken it, and will do it" (Ezek. 22:14).

O risen Lord, to Thee we pray
That on this Resurrection Day
Thy hand will part the shrouding skies
Which hide Thy face, and we shall rise
With our beloved dead, to be
Forevermore at home with Thee.

—Martha Snell Nicholson

13 Easter in Your Heart

"Mother, Easter is late this year, isn't it?" Marilyn asked, with a puzzled expression on her face.

Her mother studied the calendar. "You might call it that, though Easter could be as late as April 25 or as early as March 22."

"That's over a month's difference. Who picks the date for Easter?"

"During his reign, Emperor Constantine summoned the church leaders of his day to the Council of Nicea, in 325, and they decided that Easter should be the first Sunday after the first full moon occurring, on or after March 21."

"Sounds complicated to me," Marilyn remarked as she walked out of the kitchen.

Her mother stopped peeling potatoes and glanced out of the window above the kitchen sink at the stretch of blue sky. There were lots of things complicated about

Easter beside the date. Her hands went back to their work, but her mind went spinning. . . .

Easter should be something special. Christmas and Easter are the two outstanding Christian holidays of the year. The family should look their best at church. Her yellow nylon dress would do. She hadn't worn it much last year. She'd try to get a new dress for Marilyn so that she wouldn't feel out of things. And a new pair of pants for Hal. As for Dad, rather than something special to wear, he'd like ham and plenty of it.

But that's not enough, she knew, as she put the last potato into the pan of water and set it on the stove to cook. Easter must be more than clothes or the family would be, as the Lord had said, like "whited sepulchers" (Matt. 23:27). That was a grave that had been whitewashed. Ugh!

Easter must be in the heart! She took her Bible off the shelf, sat down in the last rays of the afternoon sun, and read of the first Easter.

She discovered that John the disciple had the true foundation for Easter. When he and Peter heard that the tomb was empty, they both ran to the tomb. Peter ran in, but John looked in "and seeth the linen clothes lie, and the napkin, that was about his head, not lying with the linen clothes, but wrapped together in a place by itself" (John 20:6-7). And John, "saw, and believed" (John 20:8). It is only when a person believes in Christ, crucified and risen from the grave, that he has Easter in the heart!

Mary Magdalene knew the fullness of Easter. When Mary went to the tomb, she was distressed because it was empty. She stayed in the garden and wept. Then the Lord revealed himself unto her and with ecstasy she exclaimed, "Master!" Jesus was not only her Savior but also her Master. She was eager to do everything and anything he wanted her to do. It is only when a person obeys the Lord as Master that he has the fullness of Easter in the heart!

The women who went to the tomb knew the spirit of Easter. When they went to the empty tomb, the angel told them, "He is not here: for he is risen . . . go quickly and tell his disciples" (Matt. 28:6-7). "And they departed quickly . . . and did run to bring his disciples word" (Matt. 28:8). It is not enough to know the Lord Jesus as Savior or even as Master. To have the spirit of Easter fully in the heart, a person must tell others that "He is risen."

14 New Clothes for Easter

A little girl, about four years old, was walking along the edge of a cemetery with her father. She pointed to the graves and asked, "What are they, Daddy?"

"Oh, they belong to the people who have gone to heaven," he replied.

She stared at the gravestones marking the different mounds of earth and thoughtfully decided, "This is where they leave their clothes, isn't it?"

She was right. This was where they left their clothes, the shell of their body, for in heaven, through Christ, they were to receive a new body. "This corruptible must put on incorruption and this mortal must put on immortality" (I Cor. 15:53).

The dead have new clothes on the resurrection morning. But we who are alive can have new clothes for Easter right here on earth. We must first put off the old garments, thankful to be able to do so, for "all our righteousnesses are as filthy rags" (Isa. 64:6). The few good deeds that you try to hold out to God: that you don't browbeat your husband, that you haven't murdered anyone, or even that you have given liberally to the Red Cross are as nothing in the sight of God. "We are unprofitable servants: we have done that which was our duty to do" (Luke 17:10).

Then, having put off our own righteousness, we can put on our new garments. First, "the garments of salvation... the robe of righteousness" (Isa. 61:10). This is our basic garment, His righteousness, not our own. We do not have to struggle to do a few good deeds to present at the throne of Christ, but rather, having no righteousness of our own, we can stand complete in him. When we accept Christ as Savior, his death on the cross as our sufficient atonement, we are covered with his righteousness.

That garment is sufficient for all eternity. But as Christians who love the Lord, we want the other new clothes which he has for us. We may be "clothed with humility" (I Pet. 5:5). Humility is the working dress of the saints. Humility is so comfortable. Once one is clothed with it, he doesn't need to strive for recognition, he needs no self-glory. He can just get in and work for the Lord. He can be janitor or lead singing. All are the same with the true Christian servant, because each is a service for the Lord.

Humility even permits us to accept blindness as did John Milton, the poet. Like him, we would then know, "They also serve who only stand and wait" because "Who best bears his mild yoke, they serve him best" (*On His Blindness* by Milton).

The Christian may also be "clad with zeal as a cloke" (Isa. 59:17). So many people are afraid of zeal: zeal for the Lord's house, zeal for his service, zeal for reaching others. But of the Lord himself, it was said, "The zeal of thine house has eaten me up" (John 2:17).

It is considered fitting to have zeal for the man or woman one loves. It is considered proper to have zeal for one's job. It should only be considered right to have zeal for the Lord of Resurrection, who gives us a new body for eternity and a new spirit for this life.

15 God in the Home

Margaret was a frequent visitor in the home of her school chum Alice. Especially did Margaret delight in being there when the family had worship. She would listen as Alice's daddy read out of the big black Book and then prayed to God. Often the family sang together and Margaret joined with them. One morning, when Margaret was present at the family altar, Alice's mother asked, "Margaret, don't you pray at your home?"

"No," Margaret shook her head sadly. You see, God doesn't live at our house the way he does at yours."

How vital it is that God's presence be daily acknowledged in our homes! Our children must know that he is in our homes. Especially is this necessary in these days of moral looseness. It is estimated that only 5 per cent of Christian people have family prayers. No doubt there is a definite connection between this forsaking of the family altar and the rising number of broken homes with all their sorrow.

It does take patience and perseverance to maintain family worship. Mrs. Webster was a widow with five children to support and train. She had family worship each evening after supper when all the family were at home.

It was difficult for her to interest her teen-age girls and her oldest son. There were times when only she and the five-year-old boy prayed and read the Word of God together. But she prayed and kept on until, one by one, the older children decided they were not "too busy" to pray with Mother.

Mrs. Webster, through a definite effort, made the prayer time interesting. Each of the children owned his own Bible. She kept a dictionary on the table and taught the children to look up words they did not know how to pronounce or did not understand. She encouraged all the children to pray.

"Let the family altar become the center around which life revolves and we will regain the spiritual resources so badly needed," Federal Judge Luther Youngdahl said. "My wife and I have always endeavored to rear our children in Christian surroundings. The unity of parents and children in prayer, the singing of favorite hymns, and the reading of the Word of God have formed the richest phase of our home life."

16 Zacchaeus Went

"Worship renews the spirit as sleep renews the body."

These words of Ralph Waldo Emerson express beautifully our need of attending church. And there is a secret to steady church attendance. It is the conviction that it is a holy tryst with God; a vigil shared by the early Christians in the dark catacombs, by the Pilgrims on the bleak shores of the new world, and today by his own throughout the world.

On Saturday night like an eager schoolgirl, you begin your preparation. You watch the clock so that you will not stay up late, for you want to be at your best in the morning. You decide what to wear, see that hubby's socks are mended and Sylvia's best hairbow is ironed. You even prepare as much of the breakfast as possible so that your mind may be free of the clutter of details in the morning, so that your spirit may be hushed before God.

There is a solemn joy in waking up with the thought, "Lord, this day I shall abandon myself to Thee, to sing Thy songs and Thy praises." And later, there is this knowledge: "I am going to worship the One who ever loves me."

An old legend is told of Zacchaeus, the publican. It tells that each morning his wife noticed that Zacchaeus was up and out of the house before she awoke. She wondered, "Where does he go so early?" and she decided to spy on him.

The next morning she awoke early, and when Zacchaeus left the house, she followed him. He went down a dusty road, out of the town. She followed, darting from tree to tree so that he would not see her. Finally, he stopped at an old gnarled tree. He pulled off a few dead leaves, weeded the base of it and watered it carefully.

Unable to contain her curiosity, she came from where she was hiding and demanded, "Zacchaeus, why are you fussing with this old tree?"

With the fire of devotion in his eyes, he answered, "Don't you remember? This is the tree I climbed to see Jesus! This is where I met Jesus!"

And that is what the church is today—the place where we meet the Savior!

17 Thanks for the Darkness

In a recent year 220 people were rescued from drowning at Pop's Willow Lake, California. Only three of them thanked the lifeguard for saving their lives!

At another resort a woman slapped the face of the lifeguard who had saved her life! She complained that he had been too rough.

Saying "thank you" never has been popular. But one who does it is surprised at how much happier it makes him—for the person to whom he says "thanks" is always so pleased, that he feels his effort is well repaid.

Those who say "thank you" easily are those who have a heart full of thanksgiving toward God. They are thankful for even the simple things in life. Charles H. Spurgeon, the great London preacher, went to the country with his friend Theodore Cuyler for a holiday. They roamed the fields in high spirits. Dr. Cuyler told a story at which Pastor Spurgeon laughed with glee. Then he exclaimed, "Theodore, let us kneel down and thank God for laughter."

And there under the trees these two men of God thanked God for the gift of laughter.

Some have even gone a step farther and have been thankful even though deprived of the things in life which we consider necessary. There was the blind girl in Scotland, who said, "If I kinna see, there's neabody in the Glen can hear like me. There's no a footstep of a Drumtochty man comes to the door but I ken his name, and there's no voice oot on the road that I canna tell. The birds sing sweeter to me than to onybody else, and I can hear them cheeping in the bushes before they go to sleep. And the flowers smell sweeter to me—the roses and the carnations and the bonny moss-rose. Na, na, ye're no to think that I've been ill-treated by my God; for if he didn't give me ae thing, he gave me many things instead."

Still others have gone on to thank God for the hard places in life. Madame Jenne-Marie Guyon lived in the days of strong religious intolerance. She dared to stand up for what she believed, and consequently she was imprisoned for many years. But of those years she said, "I have learned to love the darkness of sorrow, for there one sees the brightness of His face."

18 The Law of Kindness

Grace thought the tray was such a lovely gift. That is, until Ann saw it. Ann could have said, "I'm glad Tom gave you something pretty." But instead she said, "I have one just like it. It didn't cost very much."

The fact that the gift Grace had thought so lovely was inexpensive, spoiled it for her. Ann robbed her friend of pleasure.

All too many times we needlessly hurt one another by a thoughtless word. Ruth's husband earned a small salary, and when a dress was given to her she was delighted. But Marie made a remark to the effect that it was not very becoming. That hurt, especially as Ruth had to wear the dress. She could not buy another. Marie soon forgot what she said, but Ruth remembered it every time she wore the dress to church.

The woman who is thoughtless enough to make unkind remarks builds a wall between herself and her friends, gradually losing them. This is because, as said Pythagoras, five centuries before Christ, "A wound from the tongue is worse than a wound from a sword; for the latter effects only the body, the former the spirit."

We are inclined to excuse ourselves by saying that it is more natural for some to be kind than for others. But actually, kindness is governed by a law. When the Bible speaks of the worthy woman, it says, "In her tongue is the *law of kindness*" (Prov. 31:26).

We have to train ourselves to obey a law. Obedience does not come naturally. Remember when you learned to drive, how carefully you memorized the traffic laws, how ardently you practiced them, and how slowly you drove until you knew them.

Some drivers never do take the time to learn to obey the traffic laws. They are ever causing trouble on the road. Others train themselves, and it is a pleasure to ride with them. The same is true of the law of kindness. You can ignore it and go recklessly down the road of life, or you can train yourself to be kind.

"I wonder how Vera got her kind disposition," said Eva. "She never seems to say anything that hurts anyone."

"I think she does it by watching," explained Mabel. "She told me that she once had a terrible habit of saying sharp things, thinking they sounded clever. One day she hurt someone deeply and decided she must overcome her bad habit.

"After that, every night when she prayed, she asked the Lord to remind her of the unkind things she had said, and confessed them. Gradually, she said unkind things less and less, until now she has a reputation of being kind."

19 Medal of Honor

Carefully Christina unpinned the corsage and placed it on the lower shelf of the refrigerator. She hoped it would last several days. She smiled ruefully. Mother's Day was the only time during the year when she was given a corsage by the family. It was a special treat. It was, and she caught her breath at the thought, an honor—her medal of honor!

Slowly she closed the door and, leaning against the sink, she wondered, "Do I deserve it?" Her thoughts turned to her favorite Bible passage, "Who can find a virtuous woman? for her price is far above rubies. The heart of her husband doth safely trust in her" (Prov. 31:10-11). And her musings might well be the musings of any mother.

The most important realization that can come to any woman is that Mother's Day is founded on her relationship to her husband. That relationship is the foundation on which the home is built. It is not always easy for the "two to become one."

As the years of her marriage went by, Barbara grew ashamed of her husband's habit of wearing his clothes until they were obviously dirty.

A couple of times she remonstrated with him, but when he didn't immediately respond she bottled her resentment within her. When she was full, she began making snide remarks to him. She forgot that "in her tongue is the law of kindness." It would, no doubt, have taken many a tactful discussion to persuade him to be cleaner in his appearance, but she didn't try persuasion. Instead, she nagged. Her children grew up sorry for him, with little respect for her. Her Mother's Day corsage was a form, with little warmth.

Alice didn't nag even though her husband was stingy. Her attitude was: "No need to ask him for anything. He wouldn't give it to me." She said nothing to him but she said plenty to her friends about how penurious he was. She forgot that part of her job as wife was building up the respect of others.

Her children acquired their mother's contemptuous attitude toward Father. Her Mother's Day badge of honor was worn as falsely as a medal of honor worn by a soldier who was not loyal to his country.

Have you earned your Mother's Day medal of honor?

20 "My Mother Said"

"They say children show their bringing up, but they don't!" How often my mother said that to me when she despaired over some crude action of mine. What she did not realize was that it is not children who show their bringing up, but adults. It is now, over twenty years after her death, that I really show my bringing up.

The other night I drove a friend to a Bible class. On our return when we reached the corner near her house, she said, "Let me off here, I can walk the rest of the way."

I hesitated, tempted, then said, "No, I'll take you." Why did I drive the half block extra and make a tricky turn on a dead-end street? Because suddenly I could hear my mother saying, "Never half-do a job, especially a kindness."

The other day as I walked a path near my house, I stopped to talk to a friend. She mentioned another neighbor with whom she'd had a disagreement. I didn't especially like the neighbor either. I felt like telling my friend plenty about her. But I didn't, because I could hear my mother saying, "Don't tell everything you know. Give people the privilege of making their own enemies."

Then there are mornings when I don't feel like putting the canned milk into a pitcher or setting a plate under the fruit dish. But I do, because I can still hear my mother saying, "Use your manners at home or you won't have any when you go out."

Or the many times when my feelings yearn to be hurt, usually because something is planned and I am not included! But I can only shrug my shoulders because long ago my mother explained, "People don't mean deliberately to hurt you. They didn't omit you on purpose."

I learned not only by what she said but by what she did. Mother was a searcher for truth. True, she delved into many strange things in that search. But her heart was always searching for the answer. And so after her death I took up the search, one which thankfully led me to belief in the atoning death of Jesus Christ. I only completed a search her example started me on.

I have a vivid memory of her, with her ebony hair in a coil on the back of her neck, her dark eyes brooding, as she read her daily lesson in some book. It is true that she was not often reading the Bible. But she set an example of open-minded searching for me. I knew from childhood that it was important to take time to read spiritual books. A person didn't wait until he was tired to read a few lines. Rather, he took time in the morning or afternoon and pored over these devotional books.

With this example, when I became a Christian, I knew

that I too must keep my quiet time. It was a battle half-won because it was the pattern of my mother's life.

I am thankful for my mother's terse statements of truth and her searching attitude. I hope I am an adult who shows my bringing up.

21 Inside the Fence

Often, when you walk down the street in the summer, a sweet fragrance wafts toward you. If you pause to look inside the fence, you will see the pastel shades of sweet peas, the purple and yellow smiling pansies, the sturdy, rich purple phlox, and the pink or red roses.

The garden is well-watered and pruned. The flowers are at their best. But sometimes, just outside the fence, a few pansy seeds will have sprung up. Their stalks are stunned and their leaves withered and yellow. Weeds and grass have grown about them and are fast choking them out.

So it is with Christians. Those who attend church are the flowers inside the garden. They are well-cared for. They hear the Word of God preached. They enjoy the fellowship of Christian friends.

Those who do not attend church are like the flowers outside the fence. They have no care. Their growth is stunted. The weeds of the world are fast choking them out.

The Christian rejoices when he goes to church because his Savior went. Scripture says he went to the synagogue on the Sabbath, "as his custom was" (Luke 4:16). Jesus is our Savior, but he is also our great example, teaching us to live a full, rich life. The fact that he went to church should be reason enough for all of us to attend church.

It is interesting to note that his disciples also believed in the visible church, associating themselves with other Christians in a local fellowship. Paul traveled all over Asia Minor organizing churches. Several of his New Testament letters were to these churches, telling the members how they should conduct themselves.

The church helps the Christian in many ways. By sharing in the efforts of others, we can multiply the effect of our giving. Very few are wealthy enough to send out a missionary personally, but often the fellowship of a church can. The same is true of helping the poor. By ourselves, we could do little, but with those who are like-minded, the "littles" added together become an adequate amount.

Attending church is one way for a Christian publicly to confess Christ. He said, "Whosoever therefore shall confess me before men, him will I confess before my father which is in heaven" (Matt. 10:32). When we attend church regularly, we publicly confess our belief in the Lord Jesus.

If you feel that the church services are not interesting, it may be because you have not put forth an effort to make it interesting. After all, a church is only the reflection of those who attend it, and the effort they make to have it interesting. There is much which you can do to make your church appealing. You can study the Sunday school lesson and have a prepared mind. Or perhaps you can go early and sweep, or put the chairs and hymnals in the right places. If the piano is out of tune you could earn money to have it tuned. Or if you can play the piano almost well enough to play at the services, you can practice until you do play it well enough. Ask the Lord what he would have you do.

It has been estimated that 62 per cent of the population of the United States are church members. Yet on any

Sunday except Easter, only 30 per cent of those on the rolls attend services. Scripture reminds, "Not forsaking the assembling of ourselves together" (Heb. 10:25).

22 Happily Ever After

It was June and, as befitting the season, it had been a garden wedding. A bower of roses had been prepared at one end of the garden for the ceremony. The bride wore a white dress with a short veil and the groom, a new gray suit. After the ceremony there was cake and punch and many congratulations. And in the hearts of most of the guests was the thought, "I hope she makes him happy" or "I hope he makes her happy."

Even though most of the guests were married, all with different degrees of happiness, few had thought the matter of happiness through. They had accepted the usual cliche of "one making another happy" when the truth is, no man or woman can make his mate completely happy. He can contribute toward the happiness of the mate but happiness itself is deeper than having the devotion of another person.

Scripture is plain on this matter of happiness: "Whoso trusteth in the Lord, happy is he" (Prov. 16:20), "If ye know these things, happy are ye if ye do them" (John 13:17), "Behold, we count them happy which endure" (Jas. 5:11) and so on, in many other passages.

A couple can be happy together in the Lord. Evangelist Billy Graham and his wife Ruth are a happily married couple. They have a home, children, and mutual interests. But his preaching often takes him away from home Sometimes she goes with him, but often because of domestic responsibilities she has to remain at home.

If she were to depend upon him alone for her happiness, she would have many unhappy days because, owing to the pressure of his work, he can't devote enough time to her. But they both have the Lord. When Billy Graham's work demands that he and his wife be separated, they are still happy, because "whoso trusteth in the Lord, happy is he" (Prov. 16:20).

It is wonderful when both husband and wife are Christians and together they find their happiness in Christ. But this is not always the case. Sometimes even Christians in full-time service for the Lord are married to a mate who cannot bring them happiness.

A well-known Christian speaker, popular at Christian conferences because of his authentic Christian messages, is married to a woman in a mental institution. She has been there for over twenty years. He greatly desires to have a normal married life but this cannot be. He finds happiness in the service of the Lord. "We count them happy which endure" (Jas. 5:11).

Amy is a Sunday school teacher who plods faithfully on, teaching her class, receiving little praise or glory. Her husband is not a Christian. He is not interested in the church or in the many Christian things which delight her. She cares deeply for her husband, does much to please him, but also continues to teach her Sunday school class. She finds much happiness in the Lord because "If ye know these things, happy are ye if ye do them" (John 13:17).

23 "That's My Pop!"

"I am talking about someone who is kind, good, strong and loving," said the Sunday school teacher. "He takes care of his children in their troubles and gives them everything they need. Now whom am I talking about?"

"That's my pop!" the six-year-old yelled excitedly.

The teacher smiled indulgently. "Your father is no doubt very fine, but I'm talking about your heavenly Father."

"He's a lot like God," the little boy insisted. His theology was perfectly scriptural. The Bible teaches that a good father is the best picture of God. Scripture compares God with a father, saying, "Like as a father pitieth his children, so the Lord pitieth them that fear him" (Ps. 103:13).

The Christian dad is far more than a breadwinner. In the Bible some splendid men are set forth as examples. A good father is first of all a good husband. Joseph was such. Even when he believed that Mary had been unfaithful to him, "not willing to make her a public example, [he] was minded to put her away privily" (Matt. 1:19).

There are many ways a man can make a "public example" of his wife. Many a husband gets a twisted pleasure out of making fun of his wife's lack of mechanical ability, slurring her driving. These little digs hurt. They eat like acid. She is belittled by the one whom she wants to have the highest opinion of her. The relationship which should be her greatest satisfaction instead makes her defensive.

Also, Scripture sets forth a father as one who knows his sons intimately. Jacob's blessing of his sons (see Gen. 49) shows that though he had twelve, he knew each one intimately. He knew their character and what type of blessing would fit.

One of the most interesting things that research into juvenile delinquency has discovered is that the delinquent does not have a close relationship with his father. On the other hand, a good boy living in the same block, with the same unsatisfactory social conditions, has a close relationship with his father.

Research also proved that the discipline of the delinquent's father was usually erratic, either too lax or overstrict. In a test taken by the Gluecks it was shown that the discipline of the father was lax in 59.8 per cent of delinquency cases. When the discipline of the father was firm and kindly, only 9.3 per cent of the boys were delinquent.

The Christian father's first responsibility is to see that his son understands exactly what it means to be a Christian. Being a Christian is not like citizenship, which one receives automatically by natural birth. We can become Christians only through spiritual birth. We must be born into God's family by believing in Christ as Savior. After teaching his son this truth, the father has a continuous responsibility to live his Christian life before his son.

Faithful Christian parenthood pays great dividends. Andrew Murray was an outstanding Christian who lived in South Africa. He wrote such books as *With Christ in the School of Prayer*. Eleven of his children grew into adult life; of these, five of the sons became ministers and four of the daughters became ministers' wives. The next generation has a still more striking record, in that ten grandsons became ministers and thirteen became missionaries. Examples could be multiplied of Christian parents fortunate enough to have Christian children entering varied worth-while walks of life.

Would you have the best son in the world? Then be the best mother or father!

24 John 3:16 and Beyond

A popular quartet was singing at the church that evening. When testimony time came, the minister asked, "Will you boys give us your favorite verse?"

One by one the boys stood up and quoted a verse until it was Jim's turn. He had the physique of a football player, a shock of blond hair, and the best voice in the quartet. Obviously nervous, he repeated John 3:16.

The congregation smiled approval. They thought it "dear" for John 3:16 to be his favorite verse. But within a year, Jim had gone completely into the wrong kind of life.

It was not "dear" for Jim to be singing in a gospel quartet and yet know only one verse of Scripture. He was an example of one of the greatest tragedies in the Christian church today—the Christian who does not go beyond John 3:16. Christians must grow and spiritual growth follows the same laws as physical growth.

A child *wants* to grow. He yearns to grow. The first requirement for Christian growth is a *desire* to grow. He must want to grow spiritually more than anything else on earth, and then he *will* grow.

A child grows by eating. Most of them eat all they can at meals and between meals. A Christian grows by *feeding* on "the sincere milk of the Word." His regular meals are the church services and his quiet times. And in between times he can carry cards with significant Scripture verses written on them and memorize them. Whenever he has a spare minute, he nibbles at the Scripture as a child would a piece of candy.

A child grows by *drinking*. In the Bible, water is a symbol of the Spirit. Jesus said, "He that believeth on me . . . out of him shall flow rivers of living water" (John 7:38-39), and then the Scripture explains, "This spake he of the Spirit." One must be Spirit-taught. The two believers on the road to Emmaus knew what the Scriptures said but did not understand them until the Lord Jesus explained the prophecies to them.

A child grows by *exercise*. He runs, jumps, and plays games. A Christian grows by doing things for the Lord; testifying, singing in the choir, going with the gospel team to jail services, being an usher at church, etc.

A child grows when he is *asleep*, and a Christian also grows when he rests in the Lord. He believes what he has read and permits the Spirit to make it a part of him.

The giant Sequoia trees are estimated to be between 2,000 and 3,000 years old. They grow as high as 325 feet and are often thirty feet across. How big can a tree grow? How big can a Christian grow? There is no limit!

25 The Knot of Prayer

"Pastor, I cannot pray for my husband any longer," a wife decided regretfully. "I must give him up. I have tried so many times, but he always breaks his promise. He is drunk again."

"Don't stop praying for your husband," the pastor urged. "Keep on praying. Do your best and have faith in God."

"Very well," she agreed reluctantly. "I'll do my best but my heart is heavy and my faith is weak."

She kept on praying, and within two weeks her husband was converted. He stopped drinking and became a Christian. Suppose she had stopped praying!

Mighty things have been wrought by prayer. Elijah prayed and God withheld the rain. Elijah prayed again and rain fell. Daniel prayed and the lions' mouths were closed. Believers prayed and Peter's prison doors were opened.

Men have achieved mighty things by prayer and so can you. Alexis Carrel was a doctor and a noted man of science. He won the Nobel prize and the Nordhoff-Jung medal. He said that the more he knew about medicine the more he realized that prayer could cure when medicine could not. He declared, "Prayer is the most powerful form of energy that one can generate."

Too many of us, though we nod in agreement when someone says that prayer is powerful, don't make the effort to spend time in prayer. When Adolph Saphir, the eminent Hebrew teacher, was nearing the end of his days on earth, he said, "If I were to live my life over again I would spend less time in service and more time in prayer."

If you pray in private, it will be easy to pray in public. During World War II a British soldier was caught creeping stealthily from a near-by woods to his quarters. He was immediately taken before his commanding officer and charged with communicating with the enemy. His only defense was that he had been praying.

The officer demanded, "Are you in the habit of praying?"

"Yes, sir."

"Then get down on your knees and pray."

Expecting to be summarily executed, the soldier knelt and poured out his soul in audible prayer. When he finished, the officer said, "You may go. I believe your story.

If you hadn't drilled often, you couldn't have done so well in review."

When you get to the end of your rope, tie it with a knot of prayer.

26 Not a Great Deal of Money

Jonathan Goforth was a missionary to China and had to live on the missionary's usual small salary. In the latter years of his life he lost his sight. He and his wife returned to the United States on a small pension.

One day his wife noticed an especially thoughtful look on his face. She knew him well and said, "You are figuring how much less we can get along on, so that you can give away more."

He smiled and nodded, "Yes."

This is sacrificial giving. Giving the dollar one can spare is not the highest form of giving. The Lord praised the woman of whom He could say, "All these have of their abundance cast in unto the offerings of God: but she of her penury hath cast in all the living that she had" (Luke 21:4).

It is interesting to notice that the Bible does not say that the love of a *great* deal of money is the root of all evil, but simply the love of money (I Tim. 6:10). Some people hold on as tenaciously to a five-dollar bill as others cling to a thousand.

Some people try to claim the promise, "But my God shall supply all your need according to his riches in glory by Christ Jesus" (Phil. 4:19), and ignore the rest of the chapter. However, in the preceding verse Paul speaks of "the things which were sent from you" (Phil. 4:18). It is to the liberal that God promises to be liberal.

Pandita Ramabai ran an orphanage in India; and whenever the rice supply was not sufficient, she sent her girls out into the community to distribute to the poor the supply that was on hand. Whenever Pandita did this, God always provided enough rice to take care of the needs of the orphanage. God "loveth a cheerful giver" (II Cor. 9:7).

No doubt that is the secret—be a cheerful giver. Should anyone, having read or heard of God's generosity to others, give merely in order to get, God would know the motive. In all probability God would ignore the gift. Giving does lead to getting but the giving must not be with the desire to get—"Freely ye have received, freely give" (Matt. 10:8).

Give generously. A man was writing a check for $250 for a Christian organization when he received a telegram. He read it and said, "I have suffered a great loss. That makes a difference in my business. I shall have to write this check for $1,000.

"But I thought you said you had lost money," his friend protested.

"I did, and my loss reminded me that my Heavenly Father said, 'Lay not up for yourselves treasures upon earth' " (Matt. 6:19).

It is easy to dream and scheme what you would do if you had a million dollars. But it is probable that you will not have abundance to give from, until you have learned to give out of your penury.

Our general attitude is apt to be like the two native Christians who were discussing giving. One said, "If you had a hundred sheep, would you give fifty of them for the Lord's work?"

"You know I would."

"If you had fifty sheep, would you give twenty-five?"

"You know I would."

"If you had two sheep, would you give one of them?"

"No, I wouldn't, and you have no right to ask me that when you know I have two sheep."

Many of us would give our first dollar to the Lord, but would we give our last?

27 Your Fight for Freedom

William L. Hull, a missionary, had the privilege of interviewing David Ben-Gurion, the retiring Prime Minister of Israel. Mr. Hull brought the conversation around to the Bible. Mr. Ben-Gurion mentioned having read the New Testament and then said, "The New Testament teaching and standards are wonderful but where are those who live up to it? Are there any in the world? Are there any living the Christian life? Can this Book really produce that which it sets forth?"

Mr. Hull assured the Prime Minister that the Lord had saved him and made him a new creature in Christ.

"But are there others like you?"

"Yes, millions," he answered.

"Where are they, then? Why do they let conditions exist as are in the world at this time? Why do the nations act as they do at the present time?"

Mr. Hull went on to explain that there were Christians who tried to change world conditions. For an illustration he spoke of Lord Balfour, onetime Prime Minister of England, who when he was Foreign Secretary, influenced the British Cabinet to issue the Balfour Declaration which was the beginning of the State of Israel. Then Mr. Hull stated that there were others who practiced Christian principles in their daily lives.

But Mr. Ben-Gurion's question is a challenge to all Christians. It is one we must take to heart as again, this July, we celebrate our Declaration of Independence. If we are to continue celebrating independence we must practice Christian principles that we may secure continued freedom. Freedom is so valuable a possession that it must be defended anew by each generation.

Many different efforts are made to fight communism. One is to better the economic condition of people around the world. Much of this effort is helpful. However, it is made with a false assumption. It is done with the belief that people turn to communism because they are "have-nots."

This is only a half-truth. The inference is that people turn to communism because they do not have material possessions. Actually they turn to communism because they are "have-nots" spiritually. The leaders of the communistic countries have the best their countries can offer in material comforts, yet they remain Communists. Those who have been accused of being Communists in our country, such as Alger Hiss, or those who admittedly were Communists, such as Elizabeth Bentley, were not "have-nots" as far as money was concerned, but they were spiritually poor. They did not know the living Christ.

We must fight active communism with active Christianity, and your personal battle begins in the home. The future of the world lies in your children. The finest present you can give your country is a child or a family of children, whose Christian ideals make them upright citizens.

Seldom, however, does a child rise higher than the home which nurtured him. You cannot introduce your child to Christ as personal Savior unless he is your personal Savior and friend. The wise eyes of children see so much more than you say. If you worry about material possessions, why should your son trust the Lord for spiritual treasure? If you grudge paying your taxes, why should your son serve as policeman or mayor?

The presidents of whom we can be proud came from Christian homes. For instance, James A. Garfield's mother was an earnest Christian who taught her children that "the fear of the Lord is the beginning of wisdom." She was a widow with four children and managed her own farm. With her own hands she built a log cabin which was also used as a church. Garfield's training for the presidency began with his mother's piety.

The freedom of the world rests in the children parents are training today.

28 The Whip of Hurry

Tears filled Martha Madison's eyes. She was watching her daughter Doris take her marriage vows. Doris was a radiant bride, in her lace dress and finger-tip veil. Too, Martha was satisfied that Harry would make a good husband. Only Martha felt suddenly lonesome, as if something precious was going out of her life.

The minister uttered the final prayer. The organist began playing the recessional. The bride and groom turned and hurried up the aisle, out of the church. Martha wept. Doris was gone. She had hurried away.

Martha thought with regret of all the times throughout the years she had hurried Doris. She, like many other mothers, had hurried her children all through their childhood. She had never really taken the time to enjoy the always too-short childhood. The whip of the modern home is the word "hurry." Like a lash, mother insists, "Hurry, hurry, hurry. . . ."

This business of hurry starts with the littlest fellow. He's geared more slowly than the rest of the family. The world is all new to him, so much to see, so much to do. He is interested in only this very minute, and whatever has caught his immediate attention. A bent pin . . . a torn scrap of paper . . . a bright plastic glass . . . all are more important right then than coming when mother calls.

All too often when Josie was a little girl, she would come home at night full of talk of the day. Josie rattled, "We played hopscotch, and Daisy has a new dress and Mary is moving, and. . . ."

"Tell me tomorrow. Hurry now and go to bed."

The natural result was that the day came when Josie didn't go to her mother with her secrets. Her mother would lament, "Josie doesn't tell me a thing," when she didn't tell her about her boy friends. Then her mother would gladly have listened, but Josie's confidences had been hurried too often. She ran away and married a rather worthless boy. But he had one good quality to Josie. He had time for her.

Hurry has crept over all of our lives, even into our devotional life. The Carlburgs always had devotions before the children went to school. Mrs. Carlburg read the Bible while the others ate their breakfast and she waited on them. It was a combination of "Jesus" and "Mom, I want some more butter." Then Mr. Carlburg would pray, short and snappy, so that they could all hurry out.

If the obvious solution of getting up early enough to give the children a peaceful start for the day occurred to the Carlburgs, it was dismissed. Or they could have set aside a portion of time after the evening meal. Instead, they hurried, hurried, hurried, hurried even family worship. Then when the oldest boy, Tom, was married, he decided not to bother about family prayers. They hadn't meant anything to him in his father's home.

Scripture speaks of this tendency in human beings and admonished: "He that believeth shall not make haste" (Isa. 28:16). Unfortunately the modern tendency is to hurry the child out of the home, out of the parents' confidence, even out of the ability to live a quiet, Christ-centered life.

29 The Only One of His Kind

Elizabeth was excitedly preparing for the birth of her first child. She had bought diapers and made clothes. Her mother had given her a crib. Two showers had been held for her. And wonder grew and grew in her heart. Her very own baby! She had to do her best by the little one, and so she bought a book on the development of a child.

She read excitedly. At such and such an age she could expect the baby to crawl . . . to walk . . . to talk! She could see the little fellow in her mind's eye. She turned again to her book and read a quote from Dr. Milton J. E. Senn of Yale University. He stated, "Parents should realize that allowances must be made for a wide range of individual pattern of development. It is important that a mother learn to know her own child, rather than merely check his behavior against age traits listed in a book."

Her own child! The only one of his kind! That's what your child is. And the most important fact that modern psychologists can teach you is that God makes only individuals.

Most mothers want their children to be better than, but still miniatures of, themselves. This just doesn't happen! The child is usually similar, but he may be completely opposite. Phyllis, who teaches school and has a wide pattern of interests, had to accept as a fact that neither of her daughters was a "brain." They were sweet girls, but not brilliant. She was disappointed, but her mother heart accepted the fact, and she learned to enjoy them for what they were.

A mother can mar a child for life when she doesn't appreciate the value of what he is. Nagging a child won't make him learn, but it may teach him to revolt against books. Or belittling his ability in some lines will not increase it in another. Marcia thought it cheaper and quicker to buy ready-made clothes. It annoyed her when Geneva wanted to make her own. Marcia never fully accepted dressmaking as a necessary part of modern living, but Geneva became a dress designer with a national concern.

Only one factor will give the average mother the peace of heart to accept a child who doesn't fit her standards—and that is the realization that her child is an individual creation of God. The child did not choose his own physical pattern or mental aptitudes. Scripture says, "It is he that hath made us, and not we ourselves" (Ps. 100:3). The Bible goes on to tell us that all who become Christians were "chosen in him before the foundation of the world" (Eph. 1:4). The proper worth of each individual soul is appreciated only in the light of God's concern for each one.

Why not accept a person for what he is? God does. His interest is not limited to the talented, the clever, or even the good, for He says, "Him that cometh to me I will in no wise cast out" (John 6:37).

30 A Piece of Paper

A woman, whose name is unknown, gave a tract to Richard Baxter. He read it, accepted Christ as his Savior, and became one of England's foremost ministers. Among other Christian services, he wrote a book entitled *A Call to the Unconverted.*

Among other people led to the Lord through reading this book was Philip Doddridge. He became a minister, a hymn writer, and also wrote a book entitled *The Rise and Progress of Religion.* Through reading it, William Wilberforce came to Christ.

Wilberforce was an outstanding man of his day in England. Among other things, he fought for the abolition of the slave trade between Africa and the British possessions in the West Indies. He, too, wrote a book. It was entitled *A Practical View of Christianity.*

This book led to the conversion of Leigh Richmond, and he wrote a tract entitled, "The Dairyman's Daughter." It was first published in the early 1800's. By 1825, more than three hundred persons were known to have been converted by reading this tract. It is still being published and distributed.

What a chain of blessings came from one woman giving out a tract!

Tracts have a long history. The church fathers, Origen, Justin Martyr, and others, wrote tracts. Many of them have been handed down to us and are part of the historical heritage of the Christian church.

Tracts were one of the means used to bring about the

Reformation. Martin Luther could not go everywhere and preach to everyone but he could write tracts. He wrote many of them. The people read them and passed them on to others.

Tracts have a work to do today. They should, however, be selected with judgment. As representatives of Christ, they should be printed on a good grade of paper, with clear type. The right tract should be given to the right person. A non-Christian friend of mine was handed a tract against church suppers. She laughingly said, "Some one has confused piety with pie.

The right tract will do a work for God. A man was under great distress of soul. He knew that he was a sinner and wanted to be saved. He went to a minister, but the minister was unable to make plain the way of the cross to him. After talking to the minister, he was still not satisfied. He prayed, "Lord, I don't know what to do, but somehow save me."

As he went into his office building, a man gave him a tract and through reading it, he was saved. He never could tell the man who gave it to him. You may not know the results of the Christian literature you distribute, but you can be faithful in spreading the good news.

31 The Prettiest Bad Day

"Mommie, isn't this the prettiest bad day?" the boy called gleefully as he ran into the kitchen, water dripping from his raincoat.

"Yes, Dear, it is," Mother answered, glancing out the window. She could see the rain beating against the sprouts of grass, the wind blowing the slender buds, and the fresh beauty of the rain. Then she sighed as she thought of the years of heartache that had taught her there was good in everything, if one looked for it. All of life was a mixed blessing. There were always bugs and birds at the picnic. It depended upon the thing to which you gave your attention, the pesky ants or the singing birds. Life was continually a matter of "it's up to you how you take it!"

Isn't that the truth expressed by the teaching of the Beatitudes? "Blessed are the poor in spirit: for theirs is the kingdom of heaven" (Matt. 5:3). If you take your troubles with a gracious spirit, that is one evidence that the kingdom of God is within you (Luke 17:21). How much more important then is the spirit in which we accept life than the things which come to us.

The too-small income which keeps us from having all the things the family wants has its advantages. It should bring a man and wife together as they plan the budget, taking into consideration the true worth of the things they would like to have. It challenges the ingenuity of the couple to provide more for their children on less. Can you buy unfinished furniture and finish it yourselves? Can you make braided rugs for the floors? The handmade chair or rug will give a feeling of achievement that a manufactured article cannot give.

Even the sick child has his challenge. The weak one demands more of his father and mother, but often it is that demand which brings out the best—or the worst—in them. Lord Byron's mother hated him because he had a club foot and therefore maltreated him. But those who carry this burden with the Lord's help know that "Blessed are they that mourn: for they shall be comforted" (Matt. 5:4).

It is not easy to take disappointments, large or small. It takes a cheerful spirit to see that rain on the day of the planned picnic will give you an opportunity to do things which you had postponed. And it takes blind faith to be cheerful when the other man gets the promotion without an apparent reason. Those are the times when you have to remind yourself that in all things God works for good (Rom. 8:28).

A man came to his pastor and told him all the troubles he'd had in the past year. He exclaimed, "I tell you, preacher, it is enough to make a man *lose* his religion."

"It seems to me," the pastor replied, "that it's enough to make a man *use* his religion."

32 Spice in Bible Reading

"I have no set pattern of Bible study year in and year out, for I have found that following the same form month after month has a tendency to put me into a rut." So says Gil Dodds, an all-time champion mile runner.

Probably no problem frets more Christians and is less discussed than the problem of what to do in family or personal worship. That every one should have his own quiet time with the Lord, that every family ought to have a family altar, are accepted facts, but how to get the most out of that time is the question.

Variety is the answer.

"As a child at home we read faithfully the Bible in the accepted Genesis through Revelation pattern, chapter by chapter, day after day. Today I am using the plan of Book-to-Book reading, alternating in various portions of the Old and New Testaments and using Proverbs for one month of the year." This is the plan of Arnold Grunigen, Jr., investment banker known for his leadership in Christian businessmen's circles.

In direct contrast to this systematic reading of the Bible is the plan of Federal Judge Luther W. Youngdahl, the former governor of Minnesota. He once said, "There is a Bible in the drawer of my desk in the Governor's office at the State Capitol. My policy is to turn to chapters that have grown to be my favorites and to refer to them again and again for strength and inspiration."

Along the same line, but different, is the plan of Robert A. Cook, prominent youth leader. He says, "I stay with any particular passage in the Bible until God has said something from it to me. When I get it from him, I write it down quickly. (If you cannot write the truth down, you do not have it; you only think you have it.)"

Follow whatever plan suits you and your family the best. When you feel you are getting in a rut, vary it. Sing hymns. Music prepares the heart for worship. Give much time to praise. Some mornings spend all the time praising God for his blessings. Gratitude is as cleansing as confession. Pray much for others. Intercession is the highest form of prayer.

One young man was such a failure that he was in despair. He couldn't hold a job and was unlucky in love. His minister advised him to read the Epistle of James. In three months' time he read it six hundred times, and his life was transformed. He became an executive in a large manufacturing plant, head of a fine family and superintendent of a large Sunday school.

33 Study It!

She was sick with low blood pressure. It is one of those nagging illnesses which take the pep out of a person, yet for which there is no swift natural cure. She needed a strength beyond her own to carry her through.

Her doctor leaned across his desk with a stern but genial expression on his face. He said, "I want you to quit reading your Bible."

"Quit!" she gulped.

"Yes. Too many of my patients read the Bible and when they finish a page they don't know what they have read. In the condition your body is in, you need more than mere reading. Go home and *study* it."

His advice is becoming widespread among the doctors and psychiatrists of our day. But most of us don't know much about studying the Bible. Here are a few simple but excellent methods.

Perhaps the best one is to select a short book, or a group of chapters, and read them over and over until you know the contents. As you read you will find some words repeated over and over again. They are key words. When you recognize a key word, underline it with red pencil. For instance, in the Gospel of John, a key word is "believe"; in Philippians, "joy"; and in First John, "know."

Another way to study the Bible is by topic. Select a subject which interests you, such as faith. If you have a concordance, look up every reference to faith and by studying the reference in its context see what God has to say about it. If you do not have a concordance, read in the New Testament until you come to the word "faith"—then write down the verse and the reference, and make your own concordance.

Still another way is to buy an inexpensive notebook and carefully put the Bible verses into your own words. For instance, I Corinthians 13:1: "Though I speak with the tongues of men and of angels, and have not love, I am become as sounding brass, or a tinkling cymbal." To you this might mean, "Though I speak ever so fluently and eloquently, but have no love in my heart for others, all my fluent speaking doesn't do a bit of good."

Study the Word until you become like the man of whom Andrew Bonar told. The man said he had "*meditated* the Bible through three times."

34 Trial Is a Trust

Do you remember reading about a tornado which passed through Missouri several summers ago? The home of one of my relatives was in its path. She was standing in the living room when the roof was torn completely off, and the rain poured in, ruining everything she possessed. Her two sons were outside in a truck. It turned over, was wrecked beyond repair, and the boys climbed out of the broken glass in the door. The barns were knocked down and all the stock killed.

Yet she wrote me, "I remind myself of poor old Job who lost everything, only I didn't have the boils and I haven't lost my children. I am thankful to our heavenly Father for all his blessings, and pray for strength to come through and be a better person."

The reason Nancy could say this was because she had learned that trouble was not a trial, but a trust. When God lets deep trouble come to you, he is trusting you to bear it with faith.

Many men whose stories are in the Bible have learned this. Joseph, of the coat of many colors, was one of them. His brothers sold him into slavery. While in Egypt, Joseph was appointed superintendent of the royal granaries, and due to his skillful management, the people had food during the years of the famine. His brothers had to come to him for food, and when they recognized him, he told them, "Ye sold me hither, for God did send me before you to preserve life." Joseph knew that even though his brothers' motive had been jealousy, God was there and would work through the situation.

Bill Cunningham, noted commentator, told over the radio a marvelous story of how even the Boston night club fire of November, 1942, brought good to man. We were at that time entering a war in which many would be wounded and injured by fire. The old method of treating a burn was slow and took a great deal of care. A young doctor perfected a new method, but no one would pay any attention to him.

Then came the catastrophe of the night club fire. All too soon the remedy used in the old treatment for burns was exhausted. The doctors were forced to try the new remedy. Among those treated by the new remedy, the deaths were few. As a result, the new process was accepted and was used to save lives during the war.

God is too wise to err, too good to be unkind. Let us thank him for everything that comes to us. Even that thing which appears to be a tragedy is worth while if it teaches us to trust.

35 The Unexpected Way

The woman's children were hungry. Her husband had deserted the family. Desperate, the mother went to a grocery store and pleaded, "Please, will you let me have some food for my children? All I can offer is a prayer."

The grocer looked at her with a hard expression on his face. He felt she was trying to take advantage of him, and so he replied, "Very well. Write the prayer on a piece of paper and I'll give you food equal to its weight."

She took a piece of paper out of her worn purse and replied, "Here it is. I wrote it last night when I was watching my sick baby."

Confused because she had the prayer ready, the grocer put the paper on the weight side of his old-fashioned scales, then he put a loaf of bread on the other side. But it did not go down.

Surprised, he kept putting on food. But it did not go down. Finally, flustered, he said, "That is all the scale will hold. Here's a bag. Put the things in yourself. I'm busy."

She put the food into the bag, wiping her eyes on her sleeve between each article. Embarrassed, the grocer waited on his other customers. As soon as the woman was gone, he went back to his scale. Then he saw what had happened—the scale had broken. But he never ceased to marvel that it had broken at the exact time that he was giving food for the weight of a prayer.

God does answer prayer. "Ask of me, and I shall give

thee . . ." (Ps. 2:8). But often he answers in unexpected ways. When Adoniram Judson was a young man he prayed for the conversion of the Jews and tried to go to Jerusalem as a missionary. But he was hindered and spent his life as a missionary in Burma instead.

When he was dying, his wife read to him from the newspapers that some Jews in Turkey had been converted through the published accounts of his suffering for the gospel in Burma. He said, "What awes me is this: I never prayed earnestly for anything but it came soon or late—perhaps in the last way I could have imagined, but it came."

Another unexpected answer was received by James H. McConkey, writer of a number of devotional books. One day he was sailing on one of the Great Lakes. Suddenly the wind died and his boat was becalmed. He prayed for a breeze to take him back to shore. For about an hour he prayed, but no breeze came. Then he saw a boat coming toward him. In it was a fisherman who, seeing McConkey's boat, realized his plight and rowed out to get him. God had used not the wind, but a man, to answer his prayer.

God may use the unexpected to answer your prayer. He may use you to answer the prayer of another. If he would like to use you, could he?

When Joy Ridderhof decided it was the Lord's will for her to be a missionary, she told her mother her plans. Then she concluded, "I shall never ask you for anything; I'm going to trust the Lord; but, Mother, do stay close to the Lord so that, if it is necessary, he can speak to you."

36 For Five Years Only

When Gen Eva Carlburg held her newborn baby in her arms, she prayed, "Thank Thee, Lord, for the next five years." She knew that was all she could expect to have her son. She was a missionary and when her child was five, or at the most six, he would have to leave her to attend the mission school.

Mothers all over the United States will understand how she felt, this September. One of these mornings the little man or the dainty daughter will go off to school. Your child will never again be entirely yours. Yet, how much you can thank God for those precious five years! During them, the child, according to modern psychological findings, has learned half of all he will ever learn. It isn't only because he has learned to walk . . . to talk . . . to dress himself . . . or to play with others, but because his attitudes toward life have been shaped.

Katherine had little trouble getting her children to take a nap or go to bed at night, and, in later years, to get home when they said they would. That was, because from early babyhood, Katherine set a schedule, which, allowing for the give-and-take of the unexpected, she followed. Nap time for baby included a time of quietness for herself. Seeing her example, little Tom was more willing to trudge off to bed. Bedtime became easily established because it was proceeded by a time of family prayer. Later, when social activities called Tom, the invisible thread of a gentle routine still brought him home at the agreed time.

When Carol Sue graduated from high school and got

her first job, immediately she pledged fifteen dollars to support a little girl in an orphanage in Brazil. She was used to giving. She had been only three when her mother had given her a small world-shaped bank, and each night she had been permitted to drop pennies into it for other little girls and boys.

Peggy Ann's mother died when she was eight. Peggy Ann was lonely and bewildered. The death had been so unexpected, but after the first shock, she remembered her mother—praying, thanking God, and telling her of the heavenly home. Peggy Ann grew content, knowing her mother was with the Lord. And though some of the relatives thought how sad it was that Peggy Ann's mother hadn't lived to raise her, she never forgot her mother's training. All her life, in a hundred different ways, she reflected her mother's teaching, reminding others of her mother. Peggy Ann's most formative years had been spent in her mother's loving, shaping care.

And so, this September, when the young son or the baby girl trots off into the wide, wide world of school, don't think you're losing him. You can never lose him. You have had five years—shaping him, influencing him. He will always be yours!

37 When People See

"We have with us this morning living proof of the value of missions," a pastor said as he introduced the speaker at the Sunday morning service. "Our speaker this morning is a Christian gentleman, a convert from paganism."

The convert from India rose and going to the center of the platform smiled and answered. "Your pastor is greater proof of the power of the gospel than I. Centuries ago, when my fathers were already a civilized people, writing the philosophies of ancient India, his fathers and yours were wild barbarians, drinking wine from human skulls, the terror of the ancient world. It was when I saw what the gospel had done for the Anglo-Saxons that I was persuaded of its redeeming power."

How true it is that when people see a changed life, they believe in the gospel! When God comes into the life, it is changed, because as Scripture says, "If any man be in Christ, he is a new creature: old things are passed away; behold, all things are become new" (II Cor. 5:17). Everyone's life does not call for the same change, but the change will be there.

Mildred Comer, missionary, told of a native woman in Peru who was dull and stupid, but after she was converted, she became noticeably brighter and led her husband and many of his friends to the Lord.

Ann was a housewife who spent her afternoons playing bridge, but, after she became a Christian, she spent her afternoons studying the Bible and making baby clothes for a Christian orphanage.

Donna was a broody, discontented girl of twelve. She came to the church children's club only because some boys came. After she received Christ as her Savior, she became an alert girl and caught on to the meaning of Christian truth faster than anyone else in the group.

Bill Carle was singing at Billy Rose's Diamond Horseshoe and other such places. He became a Christian and since has devoted his talents to the church.

Martin Luther was seeking salvation through works until he read Romans and understood God's grace. Then he set all Europe free by preaching salvation through grace.

Ed Studd was a wealthy Englishman, who had made a

fortune in India. His greatest interest in life was horse racing. He urged his friend, Mr. Vincent, to bet his money on his new horse. But Mr. Vincent did not. Instead he urged Studd to come to a London theater with him, where D. L. Moody was preaching.

Studd went, listened, went again and became a new creature in Christ. He asked Moody, "Now that I am a Christian, will I have to give up horse racing?"

"Racing means betting and betting means gambling. Do you think a gambler can be a Christian?" Moody asked.

In answer, Studd not only gave up his horse racing, but changed the ballroom in his house to a hall where the gospel was preached. The change in him was so noticeable that even his chauffeur commented, "It is the same skin. But there is a new man inside."

38 Awe

Paul Hoffman was in the automobile business in Chicago in the days when only mechanics or friends of mechanics dared to buy a car. One day a veterinarian stopped by his place of business to look at a second-hand Jackson. Hoffman offered to drive the man home and much to his surprise, the car made the forty miles. In the kitchen, the veterinarian started to sign the purchase papers; then he paused and asked, "If you were me, would you buy this car?"

Hoffman needed the commission but upon the wall was a motto which warned, "God hears every word you say." Hoffman did not make the sale that day!

The presence of God has filled man's soul with awe

since the earliest days of mankind. David, King of Israel, knew, "If I ascend up into heaven, thou art there: if I make my bed in hell, behold, thou art there" (Ps. 139:8). The prophet knew that God "dwells in the high and holy place, with him also that is of a contrite and humble spirit" (Isa. 57:15).

Men have used the most lofty expressions in the human language to define God. The Westminster Shorter Catechism says, "God is a spirit, infinite, eternal and unchangeable in his being, wisdom, power, holiness, justice, goodness and truth."

"In all the vast and minute, we see the unambiguous footsteps of God, who gives its luster to the insect's wing and wheels his throne upon the rolling worlds," said Wm. Cowper, who wrote the hymn, "There Is a Fountain Filled with Blood."

"We know God easily, if we do not constrain ourselves to define him," said Joseph Joubert, the French philosopher.

These are but poor attempts to understand and define God. We can never do it because if we could, He would not be God. But wonder of wonders, this Almighty God wants our worship. Jesus said, "True worshipers shall worship the Father in spirit and in truth: for the Father seeketh such to worship him" (John 4:23).

He longs for us, not only to pray, not merely to read the Bible, but to kneel with bowed heads and be quiet while the Holy Spirit tells us of the glorious One. Robert Browning wrote a poem about a little boy who worshiped God. He wrote,

> "Morning, evening, noon and night,
> 'Praise God!' sang Theocrite."

But the boy was ambitious and began merely to say prayers instead of worshiping. God missed the boy's love, so Gabriel,

"... like a rainbow's birth,
Spread his wings and sank to earth;
And morning, evening, noon and night,
Praised God in place of Theocrite."

But God said:

"Clearer loves sound other ways:
I miss my little human praise."

This is but a poem, but it expresses the heart of God who *"seeketh* such to worship him."

39 Say "Oh!"

A new family moved into the neighborhood, but they did not attend the church services. One of the church workers decided, "I must go and see them."

"But what excuse will you have for going?" her friend asked. Then she remembered, "Oh, yes, take this book. I have heard that one of the daughters expressed a desire to read it."

"But I don't want an excuse," the Christian answered. "I want them to know I am interested in them."

So out of the kindness of her heart, she went to see the family. They were pleased by her visit and accepted her invitation to attend church. One by one all became Christians—because someone was kind.

It has been truly said, "A religion which does not make a man kind is not our Lord's religion."

Space is given in Scripture for the fact that when Ebed-melech, the Ethiopian, one of the servants in the king's house, was ordered to take Jeremiah out of the dungeon, he was kind. He took time to find "old cast clouts and old rotten rags and let them down" to Jeremiah so that he could put them under his armpits. When the rope pulled him up, it would not hurt as much as it would have without them.

Kindness is sometimes the flower in the sick room. It is the note of "thank you." It is the "please" at the beginning of a request. It is the extra moment which makes an act of duty, a gesture of love.

"It is a good and safe rule," said John Ruskin, "to sojourn in every place as if you meant to spend your life there, never omitting an opportunity of doing a kindness, or speaking a true word."

Kindness may be even less than a word. Fred was reading the evening paper when his son Freddy came into the room. He held high the finger he had pinched in the door and said, "Look, Daddy, I hurt it."

Fred glanced at the finger, decided that the hurt was not serious and said, "I can't help it, Son."

Freddy's eyes grew large and he shook his head sadly, "Yes, you could. You could have said 'oh'."

"Oh" is not much of a word but to Freddy it would have been an expression of his father's love—the balm of kindness!

Someone has said, "Just the art of being kind is all this poor world needs."

40 Warm Comfort

I lay still in the dawn-streaked room and bit my lip. In my anguish I had the blind hope that if I lay still enough, the pain wouldn't come, that the terrible process that was taking place in my body would stop, and I could save my baby. For eleven weeks I had lain on my back, but despite all the doctor could do, the pains had begun. I kept so very still, but nothing helped, the pains were relentless. I lost my baby!

Two days later, while I was still in bed, still weak, I read in the newspapers of a girl who had her baby. She had carried the little one full time and after it was born in a hotel room, she had carried the baby to the window and dropped him three stories to the pavement below and to his death. Why was her baby born alive and mine dead? She could give her baby nothing, not even a name. I could have given my baby a home, love, education, training, belief in God. Where is my answer? Where is my comfort?

"But, see," friends say, "because you don't have children, you can devote all your time to writing and thus serve the Lord."

Such words are cold comfort. Couldn't the Lord use me a little less? Does he need so much of me that I can never feel a moist kiss on my cheek? Only once have I had a friend who really shared a baby with me. Each day she let me go to her house and hold her son. Day by day I could feel the wee one grow heavy. Any talent is cold comfort to a woman whose arms are forever empty. The Bible rightly says that one of the four things which are never satisfied is "a barren womb" (Prov. 30:16).

There is one comfort when one is denied a home and family, or when he is physically handicapped. It is the simple command of the Lord Jesus, "Have faith in God" (Mark 11:22).

I do not understand why I do not have children. No service such as writing or teaching or helping others is a substitute. There is room in life for both. But the gift of children was not mine.

Then I ask myself: Is God a Father? Yes. Does God love all his children? Yes. Does he plan for them with tender care? Did he plan for me? Yes. Does he know what is best for me? Yes. The love of God for me—that is warm comfort.

Perhaps he does want all my time in service. Whatever my situation, I can say, "Amen, Lord, for 'Thou art good, and doest good'." He does need those who are not focused in few children that they may serve many. There is this one comfort in hard circumstances of life:

> "Have faith in God."
> "I will not doubt, though all my ships at sea
> Come drifting home with broken masts and sails:
> I will believe the Hand which never fails
> From seeming evil worketh good for me.
> And though I weep because those sails are tattered,
> Still will I cry, while my best hopes lie shattered,
> 'I trust in Thee'."
>
> —Author unknown

41 "A Man Has to Live"

Bernard Palissy was a glass worker who lived in the sixteenth century. The only dishes which he had ever seen were those made of earthenware. One day he saw a beautiful enamel cup which had been made in Italy. From then on, he couldn't rest until he learned the secret of baking enamelware.

He made tremendous sacrifices to learn this secret. His family nearly starved. His wife scolded. He sat by his outdoor furnace even during raging storms. He used his fence, his furniture, for firewood. He was mocked and jeered by his neighbors and creditors but he persisted until he learned to bake enamelware.

He became known throughout France. But he was a Protestant and lived when Protestants were persecuted. He was arrested and thrown into prison for his belief in Christ. However, a nobleman wanted some of Palissy's beautiful dishes and secured his release. For many years Palissy worked for the Queen of France.

Even so, the enemies of the Protestants were relentless and when Palissy was eighty he was again arrested and put into prison. The King visited him in his cell and begged him to renounce his faith, saying, "If you do not, I will be forced to condemn you to be burnt at the stake."

"Sire, I am prepared to give my life for God," Palissy answered. "Many times you have said you were sorry for me. Now I am sorry for you. You have uttered the words, 'I am forced.' That is not spoken like a king."

The King condemned Palissy to die at the stake, but

owing to delay after delay, he served a year in the Bastille and died in his cell.

Palissy was a greater man than the King because he was not afraid of the face of man. God promises, "Be not afraid of their face: for I am with thee" (Jer. 1:8).

But we are. We are afraid to stand for our convictions before men. We are afraid someone will laugh at us.

Sometimes, even our consecration is made because we are trying to please certain members of the church. We are afraid of their faces so we lengthen our skirts or wear a more somber necktie. But when you stand before the judgment seat of Christ, if your consecration was to please men, there will be no reward.

A man once complained, "After all a man has to live."

"I recognize no such necessity," replied C. T. Studd, missionary. "The necessity I recognize is that a man must die."

42 Woman with No Trouble

Rita dialed a number and without waiting for more than her friend's, "Hello," began. "Oh, Bernice, I just had to tell you. I'm having such trouble with Diana. She wants a new formal and you know with the money Harry makes we can't afford another formal for her, and besides, it's foolish for her to have two. She scarcely wears the one she has, yet she won't listen to reason. I don't know what I'll do."

"I know how girls are," Bernice said kindly.

Suddenly Rita realized her friend's voice sounded different than usual and asked, "Bernice, have you been crying?"

"Yes, it's Gwen," she mentioned her daughter. "She fell and hurt her eye. I've just come back from the hospital. The doctor won't say for sure, but he warned that she might lose the sight of one eye."

"Oh, Bernice, I'm sorry. Truly I am!" Rita flushed and felt embarrassed to her toes. How could she have said she had troubles? Diana only wanted a new dress. Diana was well and popular. Rita listened sympathetically while Bernice told her the details of Gwen's injury.

Then Bernice finished, "But, of course, I have no real troubles. After all, I have the Lord."

"Yes," Rita agreed, saying the word without thinking of why she had said "yes." But when her friend hung up, she decided that she would never again say she had troubles. There was always someone who had more trouble than she had.

There always is someone who has more serious trouble than you. The well-known saying goes, "I complained because I had no shoes until I saw a man who had no feet." No matter how difficult life is, someone else, somewhere, has greater problems.

Many people comfort themselves with the thought, "It could be worse." But that is a sour sort of comfort. It isn't being thankful that you're not as bad off as someone else. And, while it may help some, it doesn't really lessen your trouble any. Even if Bernice did have a daughter in danger of losing her eyesight, Rita still had a problem with her daughter who wanted a new dress. And it was a real problem. The lack of a dress often makes a rift between parents and children. The child may think he isn't appreciated and does things to spite his parents. Everyone's problem is real and the fact that someone else has a greater problem doesn't lessen an individual problem.

It was when Rita rethought Bernice's remarks that she found the answer to trouble. There is no trouble that is overpowering to the Christian, because he has the Lord. In the Lord there is a solution, many kinds of solutions.

Sometimes the Lord says, "And call upon me in the day of trouble: I will deliver thee, and thou shalt glorify me" (Ps. 50:15).

Sometimes He says, "Wherefore glorify ye the Lord in the fires" (Isa. 24:15).

And sometimes He says, "Wait patiently" (Ps. 37:7).

Whatever the problem, the Lord has an answer. The Christian can be like the man who was stuck in the mud on a country road. He got out of the car, took out some burlap sacks and stretched them over the mud. About that time another car drove up and the man in it called out, "Got any troubles?"

"Nope," called back the man on the roadside.

"It sure looks as though you have."

"Maybe, but I have the answer. And when you have the answer, you don't have a problem."

43 Trick or Treat

"Trick or treat, trick or treat," came the call from the three costumed youngsters when the Olsons answered their doorbell on Halloween.

Mrs. Olson smiled. She was ready. Her family had carefully prepared their treats. They had brought some children's story papers from the church and jelly beans from the store and tied the two in orange paper napkins. These were given to each child who came to the door. With the treat went the prayer that the child would read the story paper and receive some Christian help.

On an even more elaborate scale the Allyn family prepared for trick-or-treat night. Mrs. Allyn set up her Bible teaching pictures, and each group that knocked on the door was invited inside to hear a story.

By this method, each year the Allyns have the privilege of bringing several boys and girls nearer to the Lord.

Originally Halloween, or All Saint's Day, was a holy day set aside as a church festival. The original meaning of All Saint's Day has largely been forgotten in the United States. In general it has become a time of parties and pranks. In some other countries it is still a time of superstition, when ghosts are supposed to come out of their graves. In Mexico, families set food on graves, thinking the ghosts of their relatives will come out and eat.

Most of our holidays have lost their original significance. The word "holiday" comes from "holy day" and the dictionary concedes that "holiday" means, "Originally a religious anniversary, now a day set apart for exemption from labor or for a formal or informal celebration." Man, by nature a sinner, always tends to bring the finest things in life down to a lower level.

This is especially obvious in our holidays. Valentine's Day was originally kept in memory of Valentine, a Christian pastor who was put in prison and sent messages of comfort to his parishoners. Now, it has become a time of sending love notes, or even joke valentines.

The open tomb of Easter is replaced by the Easter bunny. The Savior is forgotten in the honoring of Santa Claus.

With the coming of Halloween and the beginning of the holiday season, it is time to rethink our holiday celebrations. Plan your festivities so that your children will understand their true meaning. Go to the library and get books on the holidays that tell of the origin of the day and suggest different ways of celebrating it. From these suggestions, you can select the better ideas. Then, before the Lord, meditate upon the meaning of the day and you and your family will be ready to have a Christian holiday.

44 Your Street, Your Field

The Christian knocked at her neighbor's door. When she answered, the Christian said, "We have been neighbors for several years but we have never read the Bible together. May I come in and read the Bible with you for ten minutes?"

"Why, yes," the neighbor faltered, allowing the woman to enter.

The Christian sat down, opened the Bible to Isaiah 53 and carefully read the chapter. Then she stood up, said, "Thank you," and started to leave.

"But you will come again and read to me, won't you?" invited the neighbor.

"With pleasure," the Christian answered. She had broken the ice. For several years she had wanted to speak to her neighbor of the things of God but had not known how to do it. Then she heard C. Harold Chrisman suggest this simple approach. No one resented the Christian wanting ten minutes in which to read the Bible. But her doing so awakened the interest of several, who began attending church and were won to the Lord.

Perhaps you would have liked to have been a missionary but because of circumstances you are limited to one block in the United States. So is the missionary limited to one place. He can only reach those who live near him, and you, too, can reach those who live near you.

You can pray for your street. Get a little notebook and in it, list the houses on the block. Replace the numbers as you learn the names. Gradually you will learn more and more about the people on your block. Put a check after each name as you learn if he or she is Christian. Pray for the things which hinder those who are not Christian. As you pray, you will notice the spirit of your block improve.

You can serve your block. The missionary on the foreign field does many things as a point of contact. You can water the lawn or feed the cat of the neighbor who is going out of town. You can stay with the sick while the one who usually cares for her goes on an errand. You can save paper bags for the family who take a number of lunches. You can mind the baby while a mother goes to the store.

You can be ready. "Be ready always to give an answer to every man that asketh you a reason of the hope that is in you with meekness and fear" (I Pet. 3:15). Sooner or later, the conversation will turn to religion. You can be ready. You can know what you believe. Think it over. Why are you a Christian? Why do the godly have troubles? Why is there war in God's world? Study your Bible. Consult your minister. Learn the answers to the questions which bother most people and be ready when asked.

The entire world is a field to the Lord. Your street is your field.

45 Sure Cure

Case study after case study of juvenile delinquents indicates that most youngsters become delinquents because of a lack of love in their life. Teen-agers have the twisted idea that if they can attract attention to themselves they will find an adequate substitute for love. Most of the young girls who are arrested have committed a sex offense, and always their excuse is, "I wanted to be loved." How starved girls and boys are for love!

In many cases there is little love in the home. Yet in other cases, the fault was only that the parent did not express his love to the child. Whole nations are known for "not expressing their feelings." People are actually proud when they don't! Yet, the failure of parents to express love warps the lives of their children.

Does your child think that you love him? A father defends himself by saying, "I support him!" A child takes that for granted. There are laws, both moral and legal, which make it obligatory for a man to support his children. The fact of support is not proof that a father loves his children. And mother defends herself by saying, "Think of the hours I spend washing and ironing for them." But keeping a home clean and cooking wholesome meals is not proof to a child that you love him. The child instinctively realizes that you keep the house clean because you prefer it that way—or you cook appetizing meals because it gives you pleasure to serve them.

Love is proved by discipline. True love is not maudlin. That is sentiment, and sentiment is a weak substitute for love. A child who is allowed always to have his own way misses the restraining hand of love. A child respects the strength of *no,* and responds to the love behind it. God shows his love toward his children by disciplining them, "For whom the Lord loveth he chasteneth" (Heb. 12:6).

Love is proved when you happily listen to your child. When he was a baby, you slept lightly and were awakened by the faintest cry. When he was a toddler, one cry sent you running to him. You listened to the baby. But the boy or girl needs listening, too. How quickly the retort, "Wait until you're grown up and you'll know real troubles," cuts the child. His troubles are as big as he has capacity to face and so are big to him. Take the time to listen to his problems. God has time to listen to his children. From Genesis to Revelation we are encouraged to pray to him. He says, "Pray unto me, and I will hearken unto you" (Jer. 29:12).

Love is proved in the sheer delight of being with your child. When the baby first came you couldn't hold him enough. When he was a toddler he followed you about the kitchen as you worked, and you welcomed him. But, too often as he grew older, you pushed him aside. "Go play," was an expression that drove him from you.

If you would show your child that you love him, begin again to spend time with him. Take an interest in the things that interest him. Participate—even if only as a spectator—in the things that he enjoys. Listen to music with him. Read with him. Play games with him. Attend school functions with him. God always has time for *his* children. He ever promises, "Him that cometh to me I will in no wise cast out" (John 6:37). Give time to your children and you will be richly repaid.

46 Thanks for Everything

The little seven-year-old girl bowed her head and in a low voice prayed, "Dear Lord, thank you for the food. We appreciate it. In Jesus' name, Amen."

Her mother bit her lip and patiently poured the milk in Carol's oatmeal. There had been a tug at her heart when her daughter had used the word *appreciate*. Such a long word for such a little girl! There was only one reason why she had used it: she had heard her mother say it often. And Carol's mother recognized that without conscious effort she was teaching her little girl not only words, but also attitudes.

How important it is that we Christians train ourselves to be thankful. How frequently we are encouraged in the Lord (Ps. 105:1). And how much there is for which to be thankful at each stage of our children's lives.

My neighbor was going to have her second child, and I asked her, "What do you want this time, a girl or a boy?"

"I don't care which," she replied with a happy smile. "I'll be thankful so long as the baby's normal."

The baby was. And the mother was thankful. In this day when there is so much stir to accept and help those children who are not normal, a mother should be especially thankful when her children are healthy.

All of Flora's five children were normal, and for that she was thankful, but they weren't average. That is, they didn't receive average grades in school. They were always at or near the end of the class. Flora was ambitious for her children. She hadn't been allowed to go to college, neither had her husband, and so she determined that her children should go. However, none of them received grades that showed them up to college standard. That was because their talents lay in other lines. One boy became a wizard in radio, another as a carpenter, one girl became a dress designer, and the other two daughters were "born mothers."

It took Flora many years and many hours of prayer to be thankful that her children filled their own places in the world. They didn't fill the places she coveted for them, but she learned to say, "Thank you, Lord, that you have given each one his own talent."

And there was Millie. She, like many another mother, wanted her only son Tom to marry a girl with both beauty and brains. Tom met Jocelyn at college. She worked in one of the offices. She was a plain girl but he was attracted to her. Only Millie's deep love for her son made her consent to the marriage. Five years after the wedding, Tom was afflicted with an incurable disease and Jocelyn nursed him devotedly. Millie learned to be grateful for her daughter-in-law. Both beauty and brains might have been discontented with a man tied to a wheel chair, but Jocelyn's love did not vary with his physical condition. Millie learned to say, "Thank you, Lord, for a plain girl with a beautiful heart."

Look the situation over carefully and you will find that you can "in everything give thanks" (I Thess. 5:18).

47 "O Give Thanks unto the Lord"

(I Chronicles 16:34)

Dad put his fork on his empty pie plate and leaned back in his chair. He glanced toward his wife and murmured, "Mom, you really put out the good meals. The Ritz has nothing on you."

Mom's weary face lighted with a smile and she answered, "It's work, but I enjoy getting a fancy meal once in a while. It's like wearing your best clothes."

"Yeah, it was grand, Mom," twelve-year-old Ted nodded.

"And now, kids, what do you say we give thanks," Dad suggested.

Mary Ellen, the oldest girl, looked at her father with a slight frown on her pretty face and objected, "But, Dad, you said grace."

"Sure, an extra long grace," Bud the oldest boy reminded.

"That was grace, thanks for this meal," Dad corrected. "But this being Thanksgiving Day, I thought all of us would like to tell the Lord what we're especially thankful for."

"Isn't Thanksgiving an American holiday, not a religious one?" Bud objected, with a wise toss of his head.

"Oh, that's because the men who started Thanksgiving were Christians," Mom spoke up, "and they wanted to give thanks to God."

"Sure, sure," Ted agreed.

"Okay, now," Dad said in his best head-of-the-house tone. "Let's say what we're thankful for. Mary Ellen, we'll begin with you."

Mary Ellen hesitated as if she were thinking and then slowly she said, "I think mostly I'm thankful that I'm normal. I'm certainly not beautiful like Roma Turner, or smart like Isabel Winters, but I'm pretty enough to get by, and my grades are all right. I'm thankful I'm average."

Dad smiled, "You're what a psychologist would call a well-adjusted young girl. Okay, Bud, what are you thankful for?"

Three deep lines appeared in Bud's forehead as he said, "I'm thankful that I live in an interesting age of electronics, not the old horse and buggy days."

Dad laughed, "Well, you are typical of your age, self-satisfied! But I guess, as Mary Ellen said, it's something to be normal. And now, Ted?"

Young Ted's face was serious as he said, "Well, I'm thankful I live in a free country where I can believe in Jesus if I want to and belong to his church."

"Of course, I'm thankful for that, too," Bud nodded.

"Yes," Mom said, "that's how I feel, too. I'm thankful that my children are healthy, that your dad has a steady job, that our country is prosperous. Too, I'm thankful to have a Savior and to be able to bring my children up in a free country."

Dad's face grew serious as he said, "Yes, we do have a holiday that is a mixture of religion and patriotism, because ours is a free country. I'm thankful it is, but most of all, I'm just plain thankful that I have God and his Word to show me what to do. I know that on Thanksgiving

Day we're following a principle that is rooted in the Bible: "Oh that men would praise the Lord for his goodness, and for his wonderful works to the children of men!" (Ps. 107:8).

48 Doubt Your Doubts

"Faith is a gift, but you can ask for it," said Fulton Ousler, author of *The Greatest Story Ever Told* and former senior editor of the *Reader's Digest.*

In an article entitled "My Restless Search" he told of his search for God and of the time he went into a church on Fifth Avenue, New York, to pray for the gift of faith. Part of his prayer was: "In ten minutes or less I may change my mind. I may scoff at all this. Pay no attention to me then. For this little time I am in my right mind and heart. This is my best. Take it and forget the rest, and if You are really there, help me."

Then he went on to tell how he found God. However, the point he made which is important, is that his moments of faith were his best moments.

All of us have moments of doubt and moments of faith. We have to learn to doubt our doubts and to have faith in our faith. Even the people in the Bible whom we accept as godly men and women had their moments of doubt. But they didn't continue in them. They went on to faith.

Elijah had his moments of doubt. After his great test before the prophets of Baal, he ran from Jezebel's threats. He became discouraged and prayed, "It is enough; now, O Lord, take away my life." The Lord did not answer his request. It was prompted by physical weakness, for when

Elijah had slept and an angel had brought him food, he went on to renewed faith. He had such faith in God and the future that he picked his successor, Elisha.

It was a low moment when Mary Magdalene, early, while it was yet dark, came to the sepulcher and saw the stone had been taken away. She wept. Jesus came to her and asked, "Woman, why weepest thou?"

So deep was her doubt and grief that she did not recognize him, but supposing him to be the gardener, said, "Sir, if thou have borne him hence, tell me where thou hast laid him" (John 20:15).

"Mary," he called her by name. Then she knew him and after he had spoken further to her, she went and told the disciples that she had seen the Lord. Her doubt was gone, and because she had gone on to belief, she was able to be a messenger of glad tidings.

Were you discouraged, as was Elijah, when your body was tired? Did you doubt, as did Mary, at the death of a loved one? This condition need not remain. Care for your body. . . . Rest. . . . Eat! And instead of brooding on your doubts, go on to worship the Lord. Go to his house to worship. Spend much time in prayer. From him will come faith.

"Man was not made to question but to adore" (Young).

49 How Busy Are You?

A small group of Christians stood on a street in China. A missionary played the accordion, the Chinese Christians sang hymns; before long, a hundred people gathered to listen.

Then a Chinese girl, using pictures, told the story of Jesus from his birth to his crucifixion. She told them about salvation and invited the listeners to believe in Christ as Savior. Another young girl gave her testimony, a hymn was sung, and an invitation was given to come to the services that evening.

A young man asked the young speaker many earnest questions about how to become Christian, and while she answered him, with Scripture, the others prayed.

The girl who was the speaker was fifteen! At fifteen she was going out onto the street corners telling those who had never heard the story of Jesus and answering their questions.

It is true that, to do some personal evangelizing takes effort, the sacrifice of time and the study of Scripture. But suppose someone were to offer you a thousand dollars for every person you reached for Christ. Would you make more of an effort than you do now when the reward is a crown?

The athlete wins a few silver cups and then grows old. The singer who thrills the crowd and wins their plaudits, in time, retires and is heard of no more. And so comes the end to every earthly endeavor. But the one who leads others to Christ finds no limit to his efforts in age; probably in eternity those he has won will greet him with joy. "They that turn many to righteousness (shall shine) as the stars for ever and ever" (Dan. 12:3).

Charles H. Spurgeon, outstanding Baptist preacher of the nineteenth century, says that before he became a minister, "Though I could not preach, and never thought I should be able to testify to the multitude, I used to write texts on little scraps of paper and drop them anywhere that some poor creature might pick them up and receive them as messengers of mercy to their souls. I could scarcely content myself for five minutes without trying to do something for Christ.

"If I walked along the street, I must have a few tracts with me; if I went into a railway car, I must drop a tract out of the window; if I had a moment's leisure I must be upon my knees or at my Bible; if I were in company I must turn the conversation to Christ that I might serve my Master."

"The chief business of a Christian is soul-winning."
—C. H. Spurgeon

50 "I Wish I Hadn't Done That"

Betty Lou was the impulsive kind of person who would sometimes blunder into mistakes. She was too full of life not to have done things she later regretted. But I never heard her murmur one word of regret. So once I asked her, "Don't you ever do anything you wish you had not?"

She chuckled, then grew serious and admitted, "Far too often."

"Then how come no sad tales?"

"Because I want to get full value out of my regret and if I fritter it away lamenting, it won't make me do the things I should." Then Betty Lou gave her three rules for getting the most out of regret.

First: "If you have done something you wish you hadn't, right it."

"You feel so much better if you can make things right. Perhaps you spoke in an irritable tone to someone in the home or office. If so, a kind word of apology will bring back harmony. Or, you spent all your time at the meeting with your own friends and forgot to be friendly to the new Mrs. Simpson. Go out of your way to be kind to her."

Second: "If you do something you can't make right, at least don't do it again."

"Often these things which nag the conscience are little things—like hurting someone's feelings. You cannot take away the hurt but you can train yourself not to hurt them again. Or, you told a secret you wish you had not shared. The result should teach you to keep your mouth closed the next time."

Third: "If it cannot be corrected, or used as a reminder to be a better person, then forget it."

And Betty Lou explained, "It is not easy to forget, but it can be done. I have heard many people repeat the comforting words of Jesus, 'Let not your heart be troubled,' without seeming to realize that the words were instruction for them to do something. The word 'let' implies a choice.

"You can either remember and regret or forget and have peace. It is a matter of the will. If you have confessed your sin to him, and he has forgiven you, then you must obey, 'Let not your heart be troubled.' To do less is living doubt instead of faith."

Betty Lou had learned a wonderful lesson every parent should know and pass on to the children.

51 The Only Gift

"Mommy, tell me the story about Christmas again," begged six-year-old Sharon.

"Yes, Sharon," Lelia Hammond answered. "Come, sit here by me."

Sharon settled down on the couch, comfortable as a kitten. After a while, she said, "We give gifts at Christmas because the Wise Men brought gifts to the Baby Jesus, don't we?"

"Well, Sharon, maybe that has something to do with it. Really the Wise Men did not come right at Christmas time, but quite a while later. The big thing about Christmas was the big gift God gave all the people of the world."

Sharon sat up straight. "You mean Jesus was a gift?"

"Yes, dear." Mrs. Hammond then reached out to the small table beside her chair, picked up her Bible, opened it to the second chapter of Luke, and slowly read from verse one to twenty.

Sharon's blue eyes were serious as she exclaimed, "That's beautiful, Mommy. But, Mommy, what can we give back to God?"

"Oh, many things. It is sort of a gift to him when you sing in the Christmas service."

"Away in a manger, no crib for a bed," Sharon sang the Christmas lullaby softly.

"And when we give Christmas gifts to others, we really are giving them to show our love for Jesus."

"Like the dolly we gave to Marie at the children's home?" Sharon wanted to know.

"Yes, mostly, Sharon, you can make the Lord happy by giving him yourself."

"How do you mean, Mommy?"

Lelia Hammond looked at her little girl, so young and trusting and eager to please. Lelia thought about how Sharon was growing up in a Christian home but how much help and strength and guidance she would need to face all the problems that would come as she grew up.

"Sharon, the Lord wants everyone to belong to him and to serve him. Perhaps you would feel like praying to God right now and telling him that you are giving yourself to him. Ask him to forgive you for the times when you have been naughty and help you to do better. Promise that you will live the way he would want you to. You can ask his help.

"I want to," Sharon said, solemnly. She closed her eyes. With her mother's help she prayed.

"Dear Jesus, I love You. Please forgive me for the times when I've been naughty. Help me to be good. I want to be Mommy's and Daddy's and your girl. Amen."

Tears glistened in Lelia Hammond's eyes, and in her heart she prayed, "Thank You, Lord, that she is yours. This is the best gift of all for Christmas."

52 A Truly Christmas Star

The house was quiet. The Christmas excitement was over. Under the tree was a pile of tissue paper, gay red ribbons and presents. But the last carol continued to sing in little Jean's heart. She couldn't stay in bed. Christmas was just too wonderful!

She eased out of bed, tiptoed out of the room so as not to awaken her older sister, and slipped into the hall.

She leaned over the banister, trying to see the Christmas tree, but she couldn't quite make it out in the darkness. Growing braver, she tiptoed down the stairs, pressed the switch and stared with wide-eyed wonder at the tree, with its bright red balls, silver icicles, the tiny bulbed candles and way up on top, the big star.

What did little Jean see when she looked at the tree? Did she see only the tinsel of the star? Or did she see beyond it to the star of Bethlehem? Did she see only the glow of the electric candles, or did she know, too, of Jesus Christ, the light of the world?

That depends upon what her mother and father taught her to see. For children have wonder in their souls and will see as much of the glory of Christmas as their parents teach them.

Some parents teach wisely about Christmas. For instance, Jean's parents, the Johnsons, laugh rather ruefully at Christmas as it used to be at their house—the scurry of last-minute shopping, the flurry of too much cooking and the hurry of Christmas morning celebration. Prayer and discussion have changed all that.

The scurry of last-minute shopping has disappeared before year-round, planned shopping. It begins in January with the white sales, when Mrs. Johnson buys a number of adults' gifts. It continues through the summer when, with her oldest daughter, she makes preserves to be given away at Christmas. It continues in the fall, when the boys are allowed to select their own Christmas presents for others. It does result in some of the unspoiled gifts of childhood, such as cheap perfume for Mom, and nails, "because you can use so many," for Dad. But one of the privileges of Christmas is the appreciation of the spirit behind the gift.

The hurry of Christmas morning was changed by the prayerful celebration of Christmas Eve. After dinner the

Johnson children change into their best clothes for the celebration of the Lord's birthday. They gather by the tree while Dad thoughtfully reads the Christmas story. Then the presents are opened one at a time, with many squeals of joy. After they have "ohed" and "ahed" over the gifts, they stand around the tree and sing:

> "O holy night! The stars are brightly shining.
> It is the night of the dear Savior's birth."

It is no wonder that little Jean crept downstairs to see again the wondrous Christmas tree. She had been trained to see a truly Christmas star!